Wanjiku in Global Development

Everyday Ordinary Women Livelihood Economy in Kenya

Mary Njeri Kinyanjui

Nsemia

First Edition: April 2021

Published by: Nsemia Inc. Publishers (www.nsemia.com)
Oakville, Ontario, Canada

Cover Concept by: Author
Cover illustration by: Abel Murumba
Cover Design by: Linda Kiboma
Layout Design: Bethsheba Nyabuto

Note for Librarians:

A cataloguing record for this book is available from Library and Archives Canada.

ISBN: 978-1-989928-02-8

DEDICATION

This book is dedicated to my grandparents.

Parternal Grandparents

Ngomi Mwebu was my first critical thinking teacher. Excited about learning the effects of large families on development, I asked him: *Guka niukenaga nigukurwo mwaciarirwo muri eri?* (Grandfather, are you happy that you were only two in your family?) He retorted jokingly: *thiĩ **ũrage** anyu nĩgetha **ũkenage*** (Go and kill your siblings so that you can be happy and realise all the good things).

Njeri wa Ngomi taught me to be analytical. She was nicknamed *ndemenge* due to her ability to pick up details in any conversation.

Maternal Grandparents

Juvenalis Gitaũ wa Mũchuga was one of the *mambere* or pioneers who adopted western education, money and concepts of self-regulating markets. He taught me compassion, hard work and inclusivity in societal transformation.

Josephine Nyambura was calm, forthright and a disciplinarian. By sending my mother to school, she laid the foundation for my own education.

Wambũi wa Mũnira, my step grandmother, played a major role in keeping us together as family

"This is an original contribution to women's work and empowerment, strength, power, desire, and knowledge on how to address economic, social, and political challenges."

Rose Ann Torres, PhD
Assistant. Professor of Sociology
University of New Brunswick
Saint John, Canada

ACKNOWLEDGEMENTS

My peasant family and community of Ngethu, Gatundu North, Kiambu County has always been a source of my inspiration. They face each farming season with determination and resilience fuelled by the spirit of self-reliance. They never tire to go to the farm, pick tea and coffee even when they do not know what the season will bring or what the corporations are going to pay them. Their resilience and resistance in preserving their mode of production has stimulated my desire to study similar modes of production like craft and trade. My students in the Comparative Industrial Strategies and Informal Economy in Development courses have shown keen interests in my studies of peasants, artisans and traders. Their inquisitiveness has challenged me to delve deeper into seeking for a framework for illuminating my analysis. Mr. Fredrick Dawa, the former Secretary General of Kamukunji Jua Kali Association has provided insights to this work. I am grateful to Prof. Celia Nyamweru for reading the manuscript and giving me feedback, and to Prof Agnes Musyoki for her keenness to see me complete this work. Dr Paul Kamau acted on my behalf while I was away on leave from the Institute of Development Studies (IDS). It gave me time to put into this work. I am also grateful to IDS Director and University of Nairobi for giving me a nine-month sabbatical leave and six-month unpaid leave to undertake the writing of this project at the Five College Women's Study Research Centre at Mount Holyoke. My research assistants, Kevin Gakumo, Stephene King'oina, Victor Kibet, Kazungu Makato, Symon Njenga, James Wangaruro and Perpetua Njeri played an important role in data gathering. Josephat Juma read the manuscript and gave valuable insights. I am grateful to the female respondents for their time and willingness to participate in the lengthy conversations that were part of my data gathering.

I am grateful to my siblings, Josephine, Jane, Lydia, Anna, Martin, Jimmy, Tonny, Steven and Edward as well as their families. Their moral and financial support was handy during the writing of the manuscript. My daughter, Mercy Nyambura, her husband, Moses Maina and Baby Lydia have also been very supportive in many ways.

My friends, Lydia Kamau, Faith Kimathi, Felix Kiruthu, Angela Kamau, Wambui Kirima, Anne Njuguna, Salome Mwenda, Irene Wanjiku, Helen Mungai, Debora Kyoi, Marjory Kimani, Lydia Gaitirira, Anne Kamau, Naomi Mwenjera, Neelofer Qadir, Mary Nyawira, Eunice Wanjoya , Medi Mwangi, Mary Kamau, father David Mwakiwiwi, Stella Nderitu and Francis Kanyoni were a source of encouragement.

I am grateful to my fellow associates at the Five College Women's Studies Research Centre in the 2017-2018 academic year and in Spring Semester 2019. Special thanks to Jennifer Hamilton, Director and Nayiree Roubian Programme Coordinator. Loretta Loss provided me with a lot of moral and financial support that made my stay in Mount Holyoke comfortable. She made me feel at home away from home. I am grateful to Christy Pichel and Stuart Foundation for Financial Support for part of my stay in Mount Holyoke and to Ruta Septys for her support in providing me with warm clothing. I am also indebted to Ellen Perella and Anne O'Roarks for providing me with housing and for their generosity and support in making my stay comfortable. Holly Hanson went out of her to introduce me to different communities in South Hadley. Elisabeth Ginepro and her mum Margie took me to different Catholic churches and gave me friendship and warmth. Last but not least, I will forever be grateful to the female respondents who too took time from their busy schedules to hold conversations with my research assistants and I.

FOREWORD

How do ordinary people wade through national and internal development course and practices? This book answers this question by examining the logic of life and strategies that women utilize to secure livelihood in the Kenyan economy. The book shows that, rather than being passive, *waiting for godot*, these women are proactive and innovative in their social, political and economic activities. Whereas Mary Kinyanjui reveals the resilience and exploration of her subjects based on in-depth case studies, the book is also about her own turning points in research and life. Like her subjects that she writes about, who are not waiting for the political elite to define their reality, Mary has also stopped conducting research that is solely defined for her by others.

It is encouraging to see that after persistently appraising the conventional development frameworks over the years, Mary makes a strong case for the adoption of Wanjiku's humanistic business model, articulated in the idea of *ubuntu*. This idea is not completely new. It has been in existence for many years, resisting being fully displaced by global development models like modernization and structural adjustment. The *ubuntu* model, which Mary aptly refers to as Wanjiku's Business Model, is offered as an antidote to greed, cut-throat competition, exploitation of inequality and survival for the fittest worldview that breeds conflict. Mary rightly argues that this model provides practical lessons on how self-regulating autonomous communities can work fairly and in harmony. She maintains that the model is the missing link that the modern economy needs to inextricably connect people to each other. Wanjiku's Business Model is built on the tenets of inclusivity, self-reliance, solidarity, continuous learning, democratic governance, reciprocity, pooling of resources, redistribution of resources, gifting, role of the divine, social protection, individual and communal wellbeing.

What I find rich in the book is Mary's sharp observational and analytical eye that picks up and meaningfully interprets ordinary actions and discussions, placing them in broader national and global development context, policies and practices. I greatly welcome this important work that expands knowledge on varieties of development models, with a focus on showing the contextual development of the *ubuntu* framework.

Meleckidzedeck Khayesi
Geneva, Switzerland

TABLE OF CONTENTS

LIST OF ACRONYMS

BMO	Beach Management Office
CBK	Coffee Board of Kenya
CBS	Central Bureau of Statistics
CDF	Constituency Development Fund
CDR	Centre for Development Research
DANIDA	Danish International Development Agency
DFID	Department for International Development
FSD	Financial Sector Deepening
GDP	Gross Domestic Product
GoK	Government of Kenya
HIV	Human Immunodeficiency Virus
IDS	Institute of Development Studies
ILO	International Labour Organisation
ILRI	International Livestock Research Institute
IMF	International Monetary Fund
KPCU	Kenya Planters Co-operative Union
KTDA	Kenya Tea Development Authorities
KWFT	Kenya Women Finance Trust
K-MAP	Kenya Management Assistance Programme
K-Rep	Kenyan Rural Enterprise Programme
KPHC	Kenya Population and Housing Census
KVDA	Kerio Valley Development Authority
KTDC	Kenya Tourism Development Corporation
KCB	Kenya Commercial Bank
LAPSSET	Lamu Port-South Sudan-Ethiopia-Transport Lamu
MSETTP	Micro and Small Enterprise Training and Technology Project
MRTT&T	Ministry of Research, Technical Training and Technology
MSEs	Micro and Small Enterprises
NCCK	National Council of Churches Kenya
NGO	Non-Governmental Organisation
NHIF	National Hospital Insurance Fund

PCO	Project Coordination Office
SACCO	Savings and Credit Cooperative
SAPs	Structural Adjustment Programmes
SDGs	Sustainable Development Goals
SMEP	Small and Micro-Enterprise Programme
SIDA	Swedish International Development Cooperation Agency
SACDEP	Sustainable Agriculture Community Development Programme
USAID	United States Agency for International Development
UNDP	United Nations Development programme
UNAIDS	United Nations Programme on HIV/AIDS
WB	World Bank
WEDCO	Women's Economic Development Organisation

BACKGROUND

'Our tip for the waiter for bringing us that coffee pot will be more than a week's income for the family in Africa who grew coffee.' - Richard Dowden. Director, Royal African Society. Dowden, 2010.

A majority of African women peasants, traders and artisans (herein referred to as Wanjiku) are freeing themselves from the shackles of poverty by proactively engaging in household production, reproduction and exchange. They monetise their transactions, regulate their trade in goods and services and practise gifting, reciprocity, sharing, accumulation and investing in their endeavours to realise their wellbeing as well as connect communities in time and space. They are embodiments of an anti-colonial, decolonial economy that ensures survival and connectedness to the divine, family, community and personal realms. An understanding of how ordinary women navigate production, reproduction and exchange is key to explaining the survival of peasants, artisans and traders in the 21st Century.

I conducted a research for my MA degree at Kenyatta University in 1987 on the location and structure of manufacturing industries in Thika, an old industrial town north of Nairobi. This was followed by another one for my PhD degree at University of Cambridge on the structure, role and location of small and medium sized manufacturing enterprises in central Kenya, in 1992. Following these, one of my examiners, Prof. Anthony O' Connor of the University of London, gave me a book titled *Who Controls Industry in Kenya?* (NCCK, 1969). This gesture has informed my quest to search for an indigenous model of industrialisation.

After joining the University of Nairobi's Institute for Development Studies in 1994, I engaged in commissioned researches sponsored by DFID, IDS Sussex, DANIDA and Copenhagen Centre for Development Research and UNDP. At some point, I stopped doing this kind of research and decided to conceptualise my own research topics in an effort to understand how ordinary individuals, mostly women traders, artisans, peasants, and fisher folk enter into the catch-up development model of capitalism and modernity.

My turning point was informed by five things: (a) the fact that the informal sector which is dominated by peasants, artisans and traders was not formalising and was continuing to expand despite the interventions made by government and non-governmental organisations; (b) a violent robbery I experienced when thieves attacked me in my house at Kahawa Sukari, took my furniture and electronic goods, and raped me. I attributed the attack to the increasing inequalities in the society and economy without a human face; (c) my interaction with peasants, artisans and traders not as a know-it-all researcher and development practitioner but as a consumer who realised that peasants, artisans and traders are resilient, have agency, are organised into communities and offer an alternative model of production and exchange; (d) the fact that since I am approaching retirement and my retirement benefits may not guarantee survival, I may need to go back to my village, become a peasant farmer like those that I left behind or become a trader by starting a small bookshop or something along these lines, hence doing the same activities like the peasants, artisans and traders whom I have been trying to change through policy recommendations; and finally, (e) I was curious to find out how and why peasants, artisans and traders have survived Christianisation, modernisation and liberalisation.

Due to these reasons, I began the search for an indigenous business model that is human, liberative and survives the test of time. I also look into the ways this business model is positioned in the global economy.

Christianisation, modernisation, monetisation and liberalisation have played a key role in the positioning of women peasants, artisans and traders in the global economy. Women have not only been victims of domination and control but collaborative recipients or activists of insurgency to global capitalist economy.

My lived experience in a peasant community in Ngethu village, Gatundu North, Kiambu County Kenya, as well as my role as a development scholar in the University of Nairobi have influenced the conceptualisation of my research problem and writing. I belong to the third generation of family encounter with the Christianity, modernisation and liberalisation experience on my maternal side. I am second generation on my paternal side. My family struggled to participate in these experiences with resilience and insurgency and, as a result, have maintained their peasanthood. I received western-oriented education in postcolonial Kenya. My missionary sponsored high school was headed by the Consolata Missionary Sisters from Italy. I later joined a Kenyan University where I did my undergraduate and part of my graduate training, and thereafter a British university where I had a real experience of western education.

I have had close contacts with development and academic discourses in the university, conferences and Ted talks explaining how Africa should transform or develop. I am both a specimen of development as well as a consumer of academic development discourse. This is because best practise in reading and writing demands that one deciphers and reviews literature of academic discourse.

As a specimen, I have first-hand encounter of knowing and experiencing the effects of international trade in coffee (Kinyanjui 2015). I know the limits of theory and research practice as they are applied on the specimen. For example, the theories and research practice on third world cities affects me directly because I live in the evolving self-developed urban fringes which combine the African concept of individual initiative, self-help and solidarity as well as the western city development imaginary (Kinyanjui 2019).

Living, writing and advocating for peasants, artisans and traders is not easy. To say the least, it is traumatising. It hurts to see privileged scholars churning out volumes of articles and books that keep on asking the same development question differently but giving the same answers. They come up with jargons, vocabulary, methods that change by the day but hardly solve the development question. They move from one conference or workshop to another to spread their ideas and concepts about the failure of development or more recently how dysfunctional 'Africa rising' is happening. At the other level is my lack, and that of those surrounding me, of an entitlement to a present and future of well-being. I have found myself providing moral and material resources support to people surrounding me in order to help them participate in the Christianity, modernity and liberalisation demands.

I have scars that are remnants of my personal struggle to survive modernity and liberalisation. I bear a scar that remained after being stepped on by a cow while milking. I have three scars from wounds incurred while picking coffee and tea. These scars represent my youthful agency and resilience in negotiating livelihood in a peasant background. They also represent a broader community insurgency in preserving a mode of production and exchange by passing it onto its youth. They are a constant reminder of the unfinished businesses of incorporating peasants, artisans and traders in the global economy.

My visits to Europe have put me face to face with the reality of the positioning of peasants in the global economy through international trade. While studying in Europe in the late 1980s and early 1990s, I observed that, while peasant farmers from my village were either being paid a paltry ten cents for a kilo of coffee or not being paid at all for it, the coffee shelf in a local British supermarket was always being refilled. The labels on the coffee and tea jars never acknowledged where the products came from or the farmers who produced it.

On a sabbatical in a global development institution in Europe, I came to learn about the management of African affairs. I would wonder how many people had sat on the same desk I was sitting on discussing Africa's problems while the rest of the world was moving on. During coffee breaks, I would watch delegates cool down their tempers or calm their nerves with coffee after heated debates on poverty or whatever topics. I wondered whether they ever associated the coffee they were drinking with the plight of peasant coffee farmers from my village. Addressing the issue of justice and fairness in coffee and tea trade and the production and exchange of other natural commodities would solve the problem of world poverty by 95 percent.

I have sat in high-powered meetings and conferences as well as listened to economic genius theorists on YouTube and Ted Talks theorising about the global economy and Africa's socio-economic challenges. Their ensuing proposed solutions neither address the agency, resilience and insurgency that caused my scars; the persistence of peasants, artisans and traders' production and exchange in the 21st century African economies nor the expressive outputs of the peasants, artisans and traders' social imaginaries of personal and community well-being and wealth In my endeavour to see my rural community's transformation through education, I embarked on an education programme in three primary schools from 2007 to 2015. It involved giving talks to parents, taking teachers and students for field trips, equipping libraries, and donating academic accessories such as geometrical sets to learners.

The exercise saw improved school mean scores. However, while the learners qualified to join government-sponsored secondary schools, their parents took them to neighbourhood schools. The local leadership did not support the programme and the head teacher was transferred. Some parents probably reasoned that as a single parent, I was not the right role model for their children. Others did not see in me the kind of material transformation they needed such as a big car, real estate ownership, huge business deals, political connections, plenty of money to give in form of handouts, etc. Probably, the trajectory I was recommending was too long and time consuming. I was forced to reconsider my approach of initiating transformation and the need to understand the evolution of the money culture and self-regulating markets among peasants, artisans and traders, their understanding of well-being and wealth, as well as personal, household and community flourishing.

I believe and know that education is not the acquisition of academic certificates. It is about imparting values, knowledge and skills that enhance an individual's voice and identity, hence leading to action. We in development studies seem to have missed the point when we regard education as a liability or consumptive activity. Education should aim at creating individuals who have agency. Education should aim at producing a well-rounded individual with moral and practical skills that override the primitive desires of hatred, greed for money and power for its own sake. Education transcends the mere giving of money to poor people to do business in poor localities. The current financial crisis is a testimony that availing money is not be a panacea to social economic problems.

One Sunday in February 2012, I attended a service at the Church of the Torch in Kikuyu. This is one of the oldest churches that were founded by Scottish Missionaries. I noticed a memorial plaque on the wall that hailed Reverend John William Arthur for being a doctor, evangelist and administrator at the Church of the Torch 'in darkness'. The plaque clearly implies that missionaries were duty bound to bring light to African communities in the dark. The idea of bringing light to African countries was a good justification for colonialism in the 19th Century and beginning of global capitalist expansion and modernity. It was the onset of the interactions between African peasants, artisans and traders with the global economy. It initiated them into Christianity, money and modernity. After three centuries of interacting with European education, Christianity and monetisation, why hasn't the mode of production and exchange of peasants, artisans and traders changed?

On the 24th of September 2014, I attended a public lecture by Marcelo Giugale, a World Bank Official, at the University of Nairobi. In the lecture titled *What everyone needs to know about development*, he observed that Africa is the last frontier of global development. His lecture reminded me of the 20th Century Structural Adjustment Programmes (SAPs) in Africa that led to far-reaching effects amongst workers, peasants, traders and artisans. On a personal note, the liberalisation of interest rates literally wiped out my savings. I had difficulties paying rent and school fees. I was unable to take a house mortgage. Peasants, artisans and traders reacted with insurgency and reinvented their past solidarities as they sought new sources of raw materials and markets to cushion themselves from the effects of the SAPs. Will the 21st Century endeavours to conquer or 'capture' the last frontier to global capitalist economy and modernity enfranchise or vanquish peasants, traders and artisans in the global economy?

On the 9th of March, 2016, a friend and colleague at the Institute for Development Studies, Dr. Anne Kamau, invited me for lunch at an Italian joint in Nairobi's Garden City Mall. The mall, like many others in the city such as Galleria, Junction, Two Rivers, Lifestyle, Prestige, Juja Mall and Thika Road Mall are a demonstration that we are in Rostow's stage of high mass consumption. At the Italian joint, I was struck by the furniture and pictures on the wall. Seats were made of undecorated and unpolished wooden logs fixed on metal frameworks. The lights hung from wooden canoes fixed on the roof.

The four pictures on the wall spoke volumes. The first picture had two wooden canoes and two young boys, probably of kindergarten age, by the shore. They were staring at the sea, perhaps envisaging their future jobs as artisanal fishermen. The second photo had two canoes on the shore line. A barefooted man, probably in his late 20s, sat at the edge of one canoe. He wore a *boshori*, a knitted woollen cap, and tattered clothes. He was facing the sea. Most likely, life had given him a beating. He must have been wondering whether his dreams would ever be fulfilled. The third picture featured two men sitting in a canoe. One of them adorned a white beard. He was probably in his fifties. He was wearing a baseball cap. His companion was clad in a *kamuzuri*. Their clothes were worn out. They looked tired and in deep thought, perhaps counting their losses and gains from artisanal fishing. They were staring at the sea. A young man featured in the fourth picture. He was most likely in his twenties. Clad in a T-shirt, he sat at the edge of the canoe. While the rest of his body faced the sea, his head was facing away from it. He was looking at the dry land that housed cities and towns that had shopping malls such as the Garden City Mall where modernity and capitalism are entrenched.

Should Africans be working as servile labour for global corporations which transfer profits to their mother countries (usually the global north) or go the artisanal fishermen way? Should we enfranchise or vanquish artisanal fishing? How should we position the two young boys whose future may lie in artisanal fishing not to be like their elders in the third boat or the young man looking into nothingness? These questions resonate with those of Wilson Christopher in his book *Before Dawn in Kenya.*

> "How many of the colonial communities who clamour four self-government and freedom from imperial shackles have any conception of the choice at present involved? It is not a choice between self-government or foreign rule, with the benefits of western economy as a common constant, but a choice between self-government and their own way of life with its attendant poverty and misery and oppression, or foreign guidance and the benefits of association with western economy and a slow movement towards autonomy?'" Wilson, 1952, p. 6).

Then on the 1st of May 2016, I attended the consecration of a new church at Kiriko Catholic Church. Its architecture featured an African round hut theme as opposed to the old western cathedral type. The Church had cost 48 million Kenya shillings to construct. The local peasant community had raised 40 per cent of the cost while the Holy Family Basilica Catholic community raised the rest. I compared the value of the beautiful church building to that of the dilapidated schools in the neighbourhood. In both cases, their construction entailed community participation. Why was one beautiful and equipped while the other one was dilapidated? What was more important to the community? The church or the school? What is the nature of the peasants' local imagination of where and how to use money in the community? Does spending money to accomplish matters attached to the divine realm compare to doing the same for physical infrastructure? Alternatively, how does it compare with good human education in the public realm? What lessons can we learn from the church on mobilisation of collective action in participation to solve a community problem? Why does the local catholic priest succeed while the public primary school head teacher fails in mobilising collective action for school infrastructure?

The experiences above help illuminate the discussion in this book. They highlight the importance of socio-economic justice, logic and norms of Wanjiku in production, exchange, use and value of money. The big question is whether these logic and norms should be enfranchised or vanquished.

The book investigates the positioning of Wanjiku in the global economy in the 21st Century, looking at her entry into monetised production and exchange; the role of money in her personal, family and community well-being; her logic and norms; and her nature of production and exchange after systemic exclusion by modernist and capitalist colonial and neoliberal policies.

I report the findings of this search in this book. Wanjiku's businesses are embedded in the personal, family, community and spiritual realms. This in turn affects their transactions, surplus deployment, wealth and wellbeing. Wanjiku's survival in the 21st Century is pegged on the existence of household production and exchange transactions based on solidarity, gifting and reciprocity. These attributes are key tenets of a humanist business model based on what South Africans refer to as *ubuntu,* or *utu* in East Africa or ūmūndū in Gikūyū. Archbishop Desmond Tutu (1999) observes that ubuntu is critical to sustainable development. Dowden (2010), a journalist and director of the Royal African Society reinforces that Africa's gift to the world is humanness. Wanjiku embraces this humanist economic model. The model is her gift to the current world order. We need to borrow a leaf from the way Wanjiku, who has been around for a long time, shares space and juggles with gifting, sharing and reciprocity before making panic-driven economic and political solutions to transform peasants, artisans and traders.

From Dowden's (2010) observation, we can deduce that although the global economy is universalised, it is grossly unjust and unfair to some. This injustice and unfairness should be addressed. Instead of the elite development practitioners vanquishing Wanjiku's production and exchange, they should enfranchise it by recognising that her production and exchange is not a spontaneous survivalist activity. It has logic, norms, values and structures for harnessing human agency. They should also recognise that technologies, seeds, fertilisers and pesticides should not be priced in a manner that eats into Wanjiku's meagre pay. Development elite should make Wanjiku's production and exchange visible in global consumption products' packaging and labels.

To enfranchise and position women in the global economy, a new solidarity economic model based on learning from their feminine indigenous model needs to be crafted. As Njeri Wa Ndugo, a freedom fighter from Kairi in Gatundu North observed, *Twekire maūndū maya nī getha ciana iga twī ka andū a bata mīciĩinī, matūrainī na būrūriinī* (We did these things so that our children would be dignified, generous, conscientious, self-actualising, resilient, productive, caring and judicious in the home, community and country).

CHAPTER ONE

INTRODUCTION

If we are to think of an anti-capitalist economy, we should look for it in the production and exchange done in Africa's informal economy. The informal economy operators exhibit self-determination, self-reliance, communal bonds and solidarity. They do this to actualise self, family, and community aspirations. Wanjiku, the female figure adopted in Kenyan politics and development to represent the ordinary non-elite population negotiates livelihood in peasant, artisan and trade activities as part of her participation in global development. Wanjiku resists capture and conscription into the labour and resource extraction processes of corporations and government services.

The World Bank estimates that 80% of Sub-Saharan Africa's population is engaged in informal employment and agriculture. Women comprise a majority of this population. Kinyanjui (2019) defines informal employment as the work of traders, artisans and peasants who represent a form of indigenous economy that has survived into the 21st Century. From a Marxian perspective, informal employment and peasant activities are part of commodity production that is articulated to capitalist firms (Bromley, 1978; Moser, 1978; Vakkyil, 2017). Informal employment activities take place in the household and marketplace (*soko*) in rural and urban centres. The raison d'être of this mode of production has been interrogated by many scholars. In Tanzania for example, Debora Bryceson has examined the transformation of peasant agriculture (Bryceson, 1995, 1997, 2000). Archie Mafeje has interrogated the peasant question in South Africa's agrarian transformation (Mafeje, 2003). Hart (1973); Bromely (1978); Moser (1978); Chen (2012); Chant and Pedwell (2008); De Soto (2003); and Kinyanjui (2010, 2014) have devoted a lot of time examining the same question. This book revisits the study of peasant and petty commodity production through the lens of Wanjiku. In Kenya, Wanjiku represents the ordinary low-income Kenyans who derive their livelihood from peasant and petty production. Wanjiku actively articulates peasant gender difference and indigeneity in global development. The book investigates the logic, norms and values that influence her production and exchange as well as discuss her effort to craft and articulate her economic model in global development.

Two paradigms describe Wanjiku's mode of production and exchange. The first is the Marxist perspective which claims that peasants, artisans and traders are excluded from capitalist production. The second is the modernist perspective that considers peasant and petty commodity production primitive, backward and in need of transformation to fit into the modern global economy (Dalton, 1972, Ginkel and Henkes 2003). Polanyi (1944) argues that this type of production and exchange pre-existed the arrival of corporations but was rendered extinct by the latter in Europe and North America. Today, studies on peasant and petty commodity production focus on indigeneity and how individuals articulate their logic, norms and values in global development. The studies discuss their resistance and resilience (Vakkyil, 2017) and conclude that the resistance is not spontaneous, but logical (Guha, 1983) and offers alternatives to patriarchal capitalist development (Federici, 2012). The peasant commodity production and exchange have gradually entered the culture of money and created both self and group regulating markets in their activities.

By interrogating Wanjiku's monetisation of transactions and creation of rules that regulate self and group, this book contributes towards the debate on how a majority of ordinary African women can be extricated from poverty. Wanjiku gifts, reciprocates, shares, accumulates, invests and configures households as sites of monetised production and reproduction to achieve the wellbeing of self, offspring, parents and communities. Understanding Wanjiku's logic is key to explaining the survival of peasants, artisans and traders into the 21st Century.

How has Wanjiku survived in global production into the 21st Century Africa despite the efforts to transform her through modernisation and neoliberalism? Will Wanjiku's incorporation into the culture of money and self-regulating markets give her a place in the global market? Will the integration enfranchise or vanquish her production and exchange? How does Wanjiku navigate gender differences in global development? The book documents Wanjiku's positioning in the global economy in the modernisation and neoliberalism eras. It specifically focuses on the entry of Wanjiku into monetised production and exchange, and the role of money in her personal, household and community wellbeing.

The book is based on case studies of women drawn from different parts of Kenya: Kiambu, Nairobi, Baringo, Machakos, Kakamega, Kisumu, and Kisii. The case studies provide a historical and qualitative account of the survival women, peasants, artisans and traders into the 21st Century, their articulation into global development and ability to balance gender differences in production and exchange.

While capitalism and socialism have been given acres of space in academic and development discourse, the economy practiced by African peasants, artisans and traders has received minimal attention. While the West espouses inclusive global capitalism, feminists like Gibson-Graham (2006, 2013) argue that community economies should take back the economy from corporations and globalisation. Giugale (2014) who speaks of Africa as the 'emerging' or 'last frontier' does not envision the role of Wanjiku in forging a sustainable economy. Elumelu (2014) envisions an African capitalism that evolves from corporations partnering with government through corporate social responsibility and youth entrepreneurship training.

The global capitalist economy's development does not spread on a *tabula rasa* canvas. It is spread to individuals and communities with entrenched logic and norms of production, exchange, wellbeing and wealth as well as the meaning of personal, family and community flourishing. Stiglitz (2010) and Sachs (2008) observe that the global capitalist economy encounter generates inequality and poverty. Collier (2007) in *The Bottom Billion* observes that it leaves out billions of people. It creates duality (Keith, 1973; Santos, 1979), manifests as the informal formal sector in places like Ghana (Hart, 1973), the traditional and modern economy, and also creates upper and lower circuits (Santos, 1979).

Mafeje (1981) argues that the entry of global capitalism into African peasant communities is tantamount to interference. Attempts to understand how individuals, families or communities respond to the global capitalist economy's penetration is largely influenced by an analyst's reflexivity. Awe, wonder, despair or anger often characterise analysts attempting to explain the different processes among persons, families and communities not 'captured' by the global capitalist economy and modernity. This reflexivity largely influences the conceptualisations, methods, conclusions and recommendations of the analysis directed to the creation of spaces of convergence between the analyst and the peasants, artisans and traders.

This book is influenced by the author's lived experience among a peasant community and reading and writing as a development scholar. Christianisation, modernisation, monetisation and liberalisation have played a key role in positioning women peasants, artisans and traders in the global economy. Women have been instrumental in the process of global capitalist penetration as victims of domination and control as well as collaborative recipients or activists of insurgency to the global capitalist economy.

The book's methodology is influenced by the author's reflexivity and daily encounters as a researcher and development scholar. It investigates the positioning of Wanjiku in the global economy in the 21st Century, her logic, and methods of entry as well as the role of money in her wellbeing, wealth, personal, household and community flourishing. The specific questions raised are: Why has Wanjiku's production and exchange survived into the 21st Century? How is Wanjiku's production articulated in the development of the global economy? Where has Wanjiku maintained her gender difference in global economy development? Where has Wanjiku transformed her gender difference in global production and exchange?

According to Foucault (2002), production, exchange and management of wealth and wellbeing depends on economics based on notions of value, trade, circulation, income and possibility. Wanjiku's survival into the 21st Century Africa has to do with the way she resists and articulates her production and exchange in the global economy. This in turn determines her survival.

To understand the positioning of Wanjiku in the global economy, I use case studies of women drawn from different parts of Kenya who engage in artisanal craft, production and exchange of milk, goats, art and craft, honey, fish, chicken, coffee, real estate, grains, and finance (Table 1, Fig 1).

Table 1: Wanjiku's Case Studies

Case Study	Product	Location
Githunguri Dairy Farmers' Cooperative	Milk	Kiambu
Kimalel Goat Auction	Goats	Baringo
Kienyenji chicken farmers	Indigenous free-range chicken	Machakos

Tabaka soapstone artisans' production	Carvings	Kisii
Sorghum farmers	Sorghum grains	Kakamega
Gatukuyu Coffee Farmers	Coffee	Kiambu
Dagoretti Plot Owners	Low income housing	Nairobi
Usare beach artisanal fish traders	Fish	Kisumu

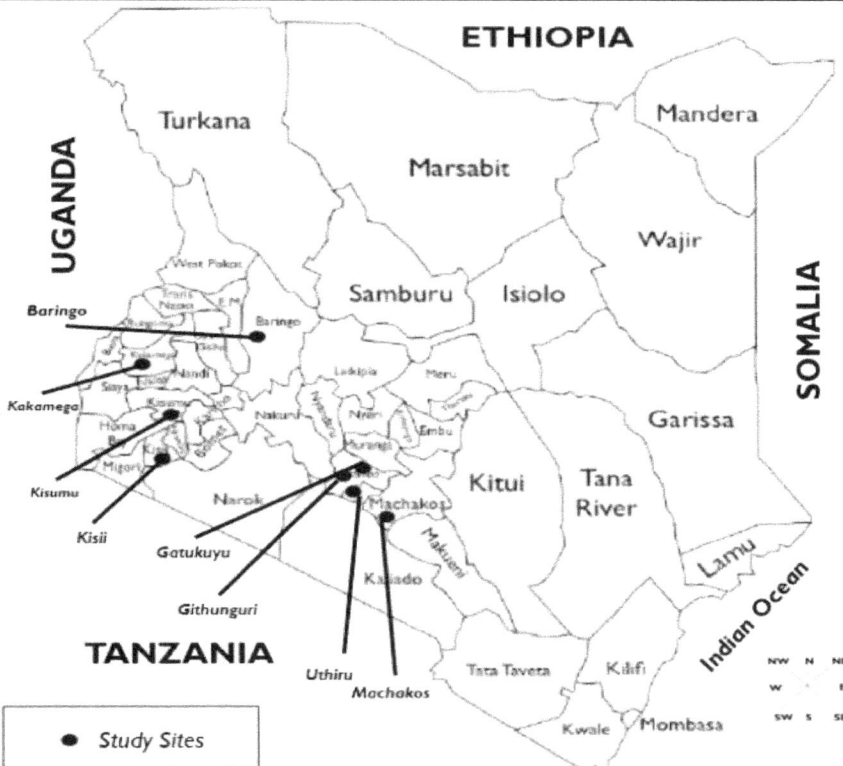

Fig. 1 Case Study Areas

My daily experiences, research capability and lectures on development studies have forced me to rethink the methodologies of development research, especially the tools of gathering data. Survey questionnaires, experimental design methodologies and statistical analysis are wanting.

Most structured questionnaires are researcher-centred. In most cases researchers seek confirmation of preconceived knowledge about a subject from the respondents instead of allowing respondents to express their experience and stories. In statistical analysis, individual experiences and stories are hidden in averages and percentages. This masks individual stories which are relevant, valid and should be heard and taken into account.

Due to this skewed approach, most recommendations arising from research do not always work. For example, while some studies hail microfinance for contributing to poverty reduction, business growth (Gyimah and Boachie, 2018) and improved consumption in health and education, there are studies that show that the recommendations for using microfinance to support the informal economy have not been very successful. Microfinance is characterised by increased cost inefficiencies (Yimga, 2018), multiple indebtedness (Shabbir, 2016), and inability to reach the poor, hence the persistence of the peasant, artisan and trader phenomenon in the 21st Century space economy.

To plug the gap, the local method of gathering information called *ndereti* or conversation can enhance data collection especially in understanding the logic, norms and values of peasant, artisan and traders' mode of production and exchange. The *ndereti* method is bound to make the interviewing session mimic a conversation that leads to building a storyline rather than compelling the respondent to narrate experiences through structured or semi-structured questions. The latter, as we have seen, ends up confirming researchers' knowledge and biases.

The method starts with establishing trust and familiarity with the respondents by inquiring about their welfare. This is followed by the declaration of the purpose of the visit to the respondent and invitation to respond to her experience in life, making the respondent to feel part of information and knowledge generation in a friendly environment. *Ndereti* minimises the feeling that the respondent is going through a time-wasting process. It gives the respondent space to express themselves rather than respond to tick-boxes in a questionnaire. In the conversation, the researcher interjects with questions for clarification. Emphasis is placed on building a conversation rather using interrogation to suit the interest of the researcher. *Ndereti* makes the respondent the centre of information and creator of knowledge. *Ndereti* creates a power balance between the researcher and the respondent. It allows the respondent to express themselves in their own terms and space without manipulation and intimidation. While researchers use their research information to confirm their objectives and hypothesis in an interview questionnaire, in *ndereti,* the respondents provide information that the researcher processes into data. In *ndereti* the respondent is the expert and generator of knowledge. The respondent reveals information from her perspective and determines the length of the conversation on the basis of her experience and expertise as the researcher listens attentively, and observes body language.

The interview may run as follows: *Habari yako? Watu wako wako salama? Habari ya familia?* (How are you? Are your people fine? How is your family?) Or in the case of a woman, *habari ya mzee na watoto?* (How is your husband and children?) *Habari ya kazi?* (How is work?) Then the weather, *mvua imenyesha sana?* (Are you experiencing a lot of rain?). In case it is hot, *jua limewaka sana?* (Are you experiencing a lot of sunshine?) The conversation begins by first addressing the person, the family, the environment, then the mode of production and exchange. *Habari ya ng'ombe na mbuzi wako?* (How are your cows and goats?) or *ng'ombe wako wana pendeza! Ungali una fuga wanyama?* (Your cows look nice! Do you still practise animal husbandry?)

The questions are rephrased and changed depending on the situation at hand. The idea is to keep the conversation as natural as possible and let the respondent speak about issues. The researcher can ask for clarification on matters raised in the conversation. For example, if the respondent retorts, *kufuga sasa ni ngumu,* (animal rearing is now difficult), one can prompt, *kwa nini ufugaji ni mgumu?* (Why is animal rearing difficult?) The respondents are allowed to have their way. In some instances, the researcher can interject and say, *hata kwetu mambo ni magumu.* (We are also experiencing the same difficulties). The respondent can then ask how and give the researcher room to give their experience.

In this book, the conversations were held in the local language or in Kiswahili. Research assistants acted as interpreters. Since *ndereti* takes time, the author focused on a few respondents from each case study who were selected purposively or by referral from people who knew them well. The objective was to hold a conversation with people who were willing to speak about themselves and spend time with the researcher. The number of respondents varied between three and five in each of the case studies (Table 1). The case studies were few compared to the number of women involved in peasant, trade and artisan activities. The objective of the study was not to generalise but to draw lessons from the individual respondents. The time spent on the *ndereti* varied from one respondent to another. Unlike the survey which is time specific that the research should be finished within, let us say six months, time for *ndereti* application and implementation is flexible and is determined by the respondent. This is because, information gathered is for lessons from the specific individual who should not be rushed to fill a questionnaire.

Chapter One serves as the introduction to the book. While capitalism and socialism have been given acres of space in academic and development discourse, the economy practised by African peasants, artisans and traders has received minimal attention. Academic and development discourse has been pulling apart on the economy practised by African peasants, artisans and traders. Approaches to Wanjiku's mode of production and exchange use two paradigms: (a) the Marxist perspective which claims that peasants, artisans and traders are excluded from capitalist production; and (b) the Modernist perspective which views peasant and petty commodity production as primitive, backward and in need of transformation to fit in the modern global economy. The case studies of women drawn from different parts of Kenya: Kiambu, Nairobi, Baringo, Machakos, Kakamega, Kisumu, and Kisii provide a historical and qualitative account of the survival women, peasants, artisans and traders into the 21st Century, their articulation into global development and their ability to maintain and overcome gender difference in production and exchange. Will Wanjiku's incorporation in the culture of money and self-regulating markets give her a place in the global market? Will it enfranchise or vanquish her production and exchange? This chapter introduces the positioning of women peasants, traders and artisans in the global economy in the modernisation and neoliberalism eras. It also explains that the subject matter of the book accrues from the author's personal journal, observations, interviews and experience as a Development scholar.

Chapter Two provides an overview of the major works on global development and their relationship with Africa. It reviews the epistemology and practise of postcolonial theory and development studies with respect to peasants and petty production because the terminologies that describe Africa in global capitalist development determine the mode of engaging with the continent. The survival of peasants, traders and artisans into the 21st Century is a sign of resistance towards the infiltration of money and self-regulating market. The chapter discusses the strengths and weaknesses of postcolonial theory and development perspectives and concludes with the proposition that Wanjiku's peasant and petty commodity experiences are not a blank slate upon which capitalism should be scripted. Wanjiku has agency, resilience and social formations that advance modes of production, exchange, deployment of surplus as well as realisation of wealth and wellbeing.

Chapter Three defines and situates Wanjiku in global development and politics. It begins by tracing the origin of Wanjiku as a concept. She represents the ordinary Kenyan citizen who is clamouring for more democratic space. Wanjiku is the low-income earner, peasant, petty commodity producer, trader, farmer, fishmonger and artisan. She represents the proletariat, indigeneity and interests of the non-elite in the Kenyan politics of global development. Wanjiku is linked to the global economy through her everyday livelihood negotiation in trade, peasant and artisan work. Wanjiku is disadvantaged and marginalised in global development despite her hard work. Through her logic and solidarity, Wanjiku has been resilient in adapting and resisting modernity and global patriarchal capitalist norms by maintaining an economic model that caters for herself, her household and community. Wanjiku's alternative feminine economic model has played a critical role in connecting people through space and time and creating flourishing households and communities.

Chapter Four discusses aspects of Wanjiku's trauma, resistance and transformation as she attempts to entrench her logic of livelihood negotiation. To understand Wanjiku's 21st Century worldview, it is important to interrogate the resistance, trauma and transformation occasioned by the processes of violence, dispossession, exclusion and isolation by postcolonial capitalism and modernity processes.

Chapter Five outlines some livelihood activities that Wanjiku engages in. Those interrogated include: goat auctions, sorghum trade, real-estate ownership, soapstone trade, indigenous chicken rearing, dairy farming, artisanry, coffee growing, and fish trade. We show that, in each of these activities, Wanjiku has attempted to articulate her logic and solidarities in production and exchange for global development. The case studies activities are drawn from different parts of Kenya including Nairobi, Kiambu Machakos, Kakamega, Baringo, Kisumu and Kisii.

Chapter Six outlines how Wanjiku articulates her logic of reproduction into global production. Majority of women were late comers into monetised production and exchange. They gradually realised that in order to contribute to human survival and thriving family and communities, they had to articulate their production and exchange into the monetised economy. The chapter documents Wanjiku's strategies to enter into money circuits. Her logic of reproduction involves the need to make money to feed her family, pay school fees, support her extended family, improve her wellbeing and reinvest. The underlying factor is to ensure human survival and a thriving family and communities. This makes the household a site for capital generation and circulation. Production and exchange is embedded in personal, community and divine realms. Wanjiku's humanism business model which combines gifting, reciprocity, nurturing, individual, group agency, insurgency, and thriving communities is a fundamental challenge to development practitioners and financers who want to leapfrog peasants, artisans and traders into neoliberal economic models. Wanjiku's structural transformation will only take place once her logic and processes of monetisation and circulation are well understood.

Chapter Seven reveals that Wanjiku's activities are not spontaneous but are structured into a collaborative and competitive model. There are rules and regulations that govern the way she does her business. The model strives to ensure solidarity, sharing, learning, healthy competition and reciprocity between the traders, artisans and peasants. It also ensures that Wanjiku's activities are ethical and harmonious. The model resonates with women and evolves through the local oratories and narratives that encourage women to engage in peasant, trade and artisan activities.

Chapter Eight demonstrates how Wanjiku uses the money earned from her survival activities to enhance her position in the household and community as well as her perspective of wellbeing. Wellbeing is viewed in multiple dimensions such as good health, good reputation, strong social relationships, emotional stability, spiritual engagement, interpersonal bonds, and solidarity. Money is not valued for its own sake. One is wealthy if she is a people-person and has agency to meet personal and socio-economic responsibilities in the household and community. Wealth is not about sovereignty and hierarchies in Wanjiku's perspective. It is about balancing mutual interests in production and exchange in the household and community.

Chapter Nine outlines Wanjiku's attempt to accumulate through her everyday livelihood survival struggles. She prefers to enhance her accumulation by investing in different ways such as purchasing and developing parcels of land, stock piling, investing in welfare groups, nurturing children and enabling other members of the community to succeed. Her accumulation takes place in the context of the household and community and is influenced by her care and nurturing logic.

Chapter Ten describes the different community economic models that have been crafted to incorporate women in global development. The models can be insurgent responses to capitalist extraction and exploitation or humanistic responses to self-provisioning and self-reliance in order to advance humanity to the next generation. A community can organically evolve or craft an economic model that facilitates its ability to survive or flourish. The model can be an insurgent response to conditions of domination and control or it can be a strategic response to its desire for independence and self-reliance. The model can be a human response for self-provisioning and advancing humanity to the next generation. A community can also craft a model through rebellion. This involves rebelling against the established order of things or going against established rules and regulations. In this case the community crafts economic models that are anti-patriarchy, anti-capitalist and anti-modernity in their transactions.

Chapter Eleven examines the lessons learnt from postcolonial and development perspectives of peasants, artisans and traders, restates why their economic mode has been resilient. It argues that Wanjiku is not a victim but an active agent articulating her production and exchange model into global capitalism. She should be given chance and opportunity to advance her cause. Wanjiku's businesses that are embedded in the personal, family, community and spiritual realms comprise the humanist business model. This model is her gift to the current world order. We need to borrow a leaf from her approaches before making panic driven economic and political solutions aimed at transforming peasants, artisans and traders. Instead of the elite development practitioners vanquishing Wanjiku's production and exchange, they should enfranchise it by recognising that her production and exchange is not a spontaneous survivalist activity. It has logic, norms, values and structures for harnessing human agency. Development elites should make Wanjiku's production and exchange visible in global consumption products' packaging and labels. To enfranchise and position women in the global economy, a new solidarity economic model based on learning from their feminine indigenous model needs to be crafted. Anti-poverty methods must acknowledge the insidious and subliminal resistance to money, debt and interest rates.

CHAPTER TWO

GLOBAL DEVELOPMENT

African (and generally 'third world') scholars should take up the challenge to rediscover themselves as part and parcel of the archaic and primitive pre-modern peoples referred to by western scholars of eighteenth, nineteenth and twentieth centuries. This rediscovery should lead to and facilitate an intellectual dialogue with the archaic, primitive and pre-modern peoples who are our contemporaries, relatives and fellow citizens (Njoroge, 2016). Global development spreads the adoption of patriarchal capitalist norms and practices. In Africa, the spread of patriarchal capitalist norms and practices began with trade but was entrenched during colonialism. Postcolonial states further embraced this form of exogenous development prescribed by international financiers such as the World Bank, IMF, and a host of bilateral development partners. Often, these exogenous prescriptions ignore homegrown and entrenched perspectives that are based on self-reliance and self-determination of ordinary people like Wanjiku. Two academic traditions namely, the postcolonial and development studies perspectives, interrogate the spread of patriarchal capitalist development in Kenya.

This chapter provides an overview of the major works on global development and its relationship with Africa. It reviews the epistemology and practice of postcolonial theory and development studies with respect to peasants and petty production. The terminologies that describe Africa in global capitalist development determine the mode of engagement with the continent. The survival of peasants, traders and artisans into the 21st Century is a sign of resistance towards the infiltration of money and self-regulating market. The chapter also discusses the strengths and weaknesses of the postcolonial theory and development perspectives and concludes with the proposition that Wanjiku's peasant and petty commodity experiences are not a blank slate upon which capitalism should be scripted. Wanjiku has agency, resilience and social formations that advance modes of production, exchange, deployment of surplus as well as realisation of wealth and wellbeing.

Postcolonial Outlook

The postcolonial outlook speaks of the transformation of the continent from colonial capitalism. It critiques the failure, corruption, inequality and bad governance in postcolonial states. At independence, African people and societies sought to produce social formations that would create dignified communities and harness human agency without adopting the principles of the colonising powers (Fanon, 1961). Colonisation had created the image of the primitive unsophisticated, superstitious, hopeless unscientific and wretched African (Fanon, 1961). Fanon observes that due to lack of capital to realise autonomy and initiate productivity, African bourgeoisies had to rely on European capital to manage the affairs of the country. The African bourgeoisies, however, failed to effect transformative change that would turn people from being simple producers of raw materials and embarked on amassing wealth at the expense of building national consciousness. Since they exploited the ordinary people like the colonialists did, Fanon foresaw the masses rising up against exploitation and freeing themselves from its strictures. Fanon advocated for the preservation of indigenous institutions, slowing down of the rising bourgeois government, political and cultural autonomy of the intellectuals, servant leadership, sovereignty, and unconditional decolonisation.

Over fifty years since Fanon made the observations, the post colony is characterised by a duality of a joint bourgeois and corporations managed government and economy in one segment, and a section of economy and society managed by Wanjiku in urban peripheral locations and rural areas. Fanon's ideals were tarnished by corruption and nepotism among the bourgeois. Postcolonial theorists like Ngugi wa Thiong'o preferred Marxism or socialism over colonial capitalism. Thiong'o (1986) argued that the decolonisation of the mind was necessary for the African to reclaim her dignity, identity and economic status. The post colony has failed because the ruling elite are corrupt (Aidoo, 1977; Thiong'o 1986, 1977, 2007). The bourgeois have resorted to accumulation and amassing of power and wealth at the expense of the masses. The ideals of equity, self-governance, and determination no longer hold. In his book *Devil on the Cross*, Thiong'o illustrates the outright theft and squandering of government resources. In *Petals of Blood*, Thiong'o (1977) clearly discusses a ruling class that has forgotten the aims of the liberation struggle: moving everyone to the centre of development. In the *Wizard of the Crow*, Thiong'o (2007) decries clinging to power, building skyscrapers at the expense of alleviating poverty, overprinting of money and pricing projects highly.

In *Secure the Base: Making Africa Visible in the Globe*, Thiong'o (2016) argues that there are still unanswered questions and issues that need to be addressed with regard to Africa's position as an underdeveloped continent in the global framework. In one of the essays in the book: 'Privatise or be Damned,' Thiong'o pokes holes on privatisation as a solution for economic development in Africa and recommends the creation of meaningful dialogue and equal exchange between countries in economic, political, cultural and psychic realms.

> "The wholeness can never be any but that which is rooted in the people - not the middle class. I see all these as the interrelated complexity we call human societies as opposed to the current forms of globalisation that often mean the appropriation of all the other centres and their resources to serve one super centre." (Thiong'o, 2016:59).

Thiong'o differentiates globalisation of finance capital, which creates a glossy middle class, from globalism, which creates a prosperous creative people, their common humanity expressed in multicoloured particularities (Thiong'o, 2016:60). Real development includes the creativity, resilience and particularities of Wanjiku in the global framework.

Ama Ata Aidoo (1977) also decries African leaders who concentrate on personal wealth accumulation instead of driving development. Her poem Our Sister Killjoy argues that Third World leaders in general and African ones in particular are apparently asleep all the time. They do not give a damn to development and welfare of the people.

> Our Sister Killjoy by Ama Ata Aidoo
>
> "From all around the Third World,
> You hear the same story;
> Rulers
> Asleep to all things at
> All times -
> Conscious only of
> Riches, which they gather in a
> Coma -
> Intravenously

So that
You wouldn't know they were
Feeding if it was not for the
Occasional
Tell-tale trickle somewhere
Around the mouth.
And when they are jolted awake,
They stare about them with
Unseeing eyes, just
Sleep walkers in a nightmare."

The call for an African identity is another issue addressed by postcolonial theorists. Mazrui (1963; 1986) advances the quest for an African identity in the global arena. Who is an African? Is an African defined by geographical status or relationship with Europe? According to Mazrui, the African's encounter with western and Islamic cultures has a bearing on African identity. In one of his writings in the *Journal of Association of American Political Scientists*, Mazrui (1986) explored Nkrumah's concept of *We are all Africans*. Nkrumah opposed an Africa that was an extension of Europe. Mazrui in his video and book *The Africans: A Triple Heritage* argues that the African post colony is a product of a triple heritage that encompasses African traditional experience, Western European experience and Islamic influence. The triple heritage needs to be deconstructed and nuanced in academic development discourse. This book does this by interrogating the positioning of Wanjiku globally.

From the narrations of most postcolonial theorists, it is clear that African leaders who replaced colonial government administration and corporate boardrooms did little to introduce inclusive transformation of society. The leaders did not evolve creative strategies and philosophies that would incorporate ordinary people in the economy and governance. They perpetuated the appropriation of surplus and control of ordinary people. They did not preserve and advance indigenous institutions as envisioned by Fanon. Wanjiku was left on her own to devise and craft strategies for personal and community survival. Wanjiku drew on the solidarities and past experiences to evolve an economic model that ensured survival amidst control, domination and exploitation.

Some scholars like Bryceson (1995, 1997); Chant (2016) and Chen (2012) discuss the rise of precarious work conditions in the unorganised sector of the post colony, de-peasantisation, creation of footloose labour; the rise of the household as the new site of capitalist production and market system; and the growth of affective labour. The rise of the household as the new site for capitalist production, market system and the growth of affective labour are of relevance to this book that advocates for the integration and articulation of Wanjiku in the global economy. How is Wanjiku's base of production and exchange? How does Wanjiku navigate the process of accumulation in the context of de-peasantisation and dislocation due to the expansion of the bourgeois, state and corporation accumulation?

Development Studies Outlook

Most development strategies in Africa are externally generated and largely supported by financiers such as the World Bank, the International Monetary Fund and a series of multilateral and bilateral donors. Development projects have involved grandiose projects aimed at revolutionising peasant agriculture and improving physical infrastructure. In Kenya, the government has initiated programmes to move farmers from producing for subsistence. The programmes include: setting up agricultural research institutes, agribusiness programmes in university curriculums, farmer training and extension services, demonstration farms, finance provision, creation of marketing boards and fertiliser subsidy. Agriculture and small enterprise-related bills have been enacted to promote businesses in the informal sector. The private sector has initiated programmes for contract farming, for example, in poultry. The World Bank and the USAID in their support for structural transformation of small farmers fund Government and NGOs that engage in linking small-scale farmers to technology, markets, and improved seeds. Unfortunately, results from these initiatives have been disappointing. The economic models have not been very effective. Peasant production and the informal economy thus persist in Africa in the 21st Century (Kinyanjui, 2014, 2019; Caretta and Cheptum, 2019).

Development Studies Perspective

Development scholars have discussed the failure to transform Wanjiku through grand projects. Hyden (1980) acknowledges that development policies, state interventions, and market driven structural adjustment programmes failed to capture the peasants. He calls for proactive policies that transform the economies of affection into market-based production and exchange. Giugale (2014) observes that the use of technology, democracy and wealth distribution will incorporate Africa into the capitalist global development.

The terminologies that describe Africa in global capitalist development determine the modes of engaging with the continent. Terminologies like 'Dark Continent' and 'Virgin Continent' that preceded Africa's colonial engagement determined the economic and political strategies that were used to tackle traditional structures and the unexploited or unexplored resources in the continent. In a bid to bring 'light' to a 'dark continent', domination and control were deployed, leaving the African with limited latitude to take part in charting the course of development. With the prevailing extraction and exportation of resources to Europe, Africans were turned into mass consumers of imported commodities. Local production was stifled as African production methods were replaced with imported ones. After three centuries of 'bringing light' to the continent through plunder and acculturation, Africa unfortunately became the least developed of all the continents. After decades of colonisation, Africa occupied a subservient position where it relied on capital, technology and knowledge for development from Europe and North America.

At independence, African leaders and scholars were preoccupied with the question of how to configure the African postcolonial state. Leaders like Tom Mboya (1970) observed that Europeans moved out of Africa so that Africans would put it together. He also noted that Africans must negotiate with Europeans on equal basis. According to Mboya, as long as any part of Africa was under European rule, Africans would always be unfairly cast.

Lewis (1954) in his investigation of the problems of distribution, accumulation and growth in Africa observes that the African economy is made of two sectors: (a) the capitalist and the non-capitalist, and (b) the modern and the non-modern.

The capitalist economic sector uses capital and hires labour to reproduce capital. Financial institutions are also fairly well developed. The non-capitalist sector mainly produces for subsistence. The marginal productivity of labour in the non-capitalist sector is negligible, zero or negative. It is characterised by disguised unemployment, casual workers, gardeners, petty trading and domestic services. The wages are small and used for subsistence. The non-capitalist sector serves as the reservoir of labour for the capitalist sector. Population growth ensures that there is unlimited supply of labour. For a long time, development was seen in terms of bringing people from the non-capitalist sector to the capitalist one. This kind of thinking has largely influenced most of the development work carried out by African government and international development practitioners.

Todaro's (1994) in the book *Economic Development* argues that poverty, inequality, unemployment, population growth, environmental decay, rural stagnation and violent conflict stifle economic development. For example, the high population growth impacts on rural urban migration, contributes to unemployment and increases government expenditure on service delivery. Thus, for economic development to take place, population growth has to be addressed. This informs the bid to control birth rates through family planning and the establishment of population studies and advisory institutes.

In 1983, Hyden's book *No Shortcuts to Africa's Progress* argued that Africa needed to take hard options to spur development. This meant addressing the issue of economies of affection and public administration. During the same period, the World Bank and IMF package of structural adjustments provided a road map to correct market inefficiencies through liberalisation. The ensuing opening up of markets exposed locally produced goods in Africa to global competition. The World Bank and IMF also recommended the opening up of the democratic space to create competitive politics; the recognition of individual property rights to spur creativity and entrepreneurship; the restructuring of the public service to make it lean; the provision of incentives to civil servants in terms of high wages to curtail corruption; currency reforms, and reduction of government expenditure through privatisation of government-owned industries and services and cost-sharing measures. Essentially, structural adjustment programmes took away the socialist social formations in the postcolonial state and replaced them with capitalist ideologies. Structural adjustment programmes contributed to rising inequalities and financial crises that affected a large majority of ordinary people (Rono, 2002).

Development scholars acknowledge that all is not well with the capitalist global economy. Stiglitz (2010) calls for revised contracts between the citizens and government. One contract that should be revised is the one involving women peasants, artisans and traders with African governments, international development practitioners and financiers. Stiglitz (2010) is a proponent of an inclusive and sustainable global economy. He argues that the United States of America and China must acknowledge that the market fundamentals of the pre-2008 period have not worked and that self-regulating markets have limitations. Development will only be possible through the creation of new social contracts between all the elements of society such as citizens and governments. Sachs (2008) considers the restructuring of the global economy as an urgent phenomenon and calls for greater cooperation between countries, the provision of financial aid to poor continents and vibrancy of civil societies and corporations to drive change.

States, individuals trained in the west, financial capital and foreign corporations extend global capitalism in non-traditional areas like India, Asia, China, and Argentina. Globalisation has presented a trilemma in most parts of the globe (Rodrick, 2011). Financial crises have been experienced in Asia and Argentina making globalisation seem untenable in the 21st Century.

Critiquing the grand development projects financed by donor aid, Booth and Cammack (2013) observe that the failure of development aid to bring change in Africa is attributable to the failure by communities to use collective action to solve their everyday problems. Booth and Cammack's conclusions are drawn from studies done in Rwanda, Mali, Niger and Uganda. Stiglitz, Sachs, Booth and Cammack do not attribute Africa's problems to effects of free markets, individual interest, exploitation and extraction of resources from the continent.

Some development scholars have made specific proposals for global development in Africa. Page (2012) calls for the structural transformation of traders, artisans and small scale peasant producers in order for Africans to become part of the globalised world. He believes that informality has been the drawback curtailing African development. Mahajan (2008) in Africa Rising recommends that Africa's development should be driven by the youth since they constitute a major driving force for the economy, as well as a market for consumer goods. He also proposes the intensification of foreign capital investments by global corporations in the continent.

Observations on Africa's potential for global development are also made by (Elumelu 2014) who observes that there is great potential in Africa for private sector-led investments in what he calls Africapitalism. In Africapitalism, African companies make money and invest in social and physical infrastructure. Noting that Africapitalism will evolve through a new cadre of leadership driven by the youth, he has initiated a youth entrepreneurship and leadership initiative. Thandika Mkandawire (2010, 2014, 2015) proposes an elite-led development agenda in Africa. He uses President Julius Nyerere's memento that 'Africa must run while others walk' in order to catch up with the capitalist global development. Mkandawire considers Africa's catch-up development model as slow and unfruitful due to its failure to include the elite in the development process, and its disregard for the role of the universities and other institutes of research and hogher learning in generating knowledge for development. In a 2014 article titled *'The Spread of Policy Making and Economic Doctrine in Post Colonial Africa'* Mkandawire demonstrates how development ideas have evolved. After independence (1960 to 1970), African governments introduced structuralist-developmentalist and neo-Marxist perspectives where they planned and participated in development through large-scale parastatal-led investments. The governments also introduced welfarist policies in education and health. In the 1980s to 1990s, African governments under the instruction of the World Bank and the International Monetary Fund introduced neoliberal policies. The main idea was to take back the structuralist development state and introduce market-based reforms. The policies involved African governments disinvesting from economic development, privatising, removing protections and liberalising trade and financial infrastructure, cost-sharing in health and education, as well as reducing wage bills by retrenching workers in the civil service. This structural adjustments phase was followed by institutional reforms that included democratisation, introduction of multiparty politics, poverty reduction strategies, addressing slum poverty and providing cash transfers to the elderly.

Mkandawire, (2015) in his personal reflections on the fifty years of African independence, underscores that the process of African development is relatively complex. He starts by pointing at the young generation's amnesia of the historical origins of the current social, economic and political problems. He questions the African leaders' expectations of independence. Ghanaian President Nkrumah's vision was one of gaining political independence, while that of Dr. Kamuzu Banda from Malawi was attaining peace and working hard. President Jomo Kenyatta of Kenya acknowledged that there was no free lunch and advocated for freedom and hard work. Mkandawire acknowledges that across Africa countries experienced significant handicaps in creating new nations, developing national identities, constrained by neocolonialism and with no clarity on which development model to follow. They were caught in between, on the one hand, the Truman Doctrine which emphasised the need for foreign aid. On the other hand was the Bandung conference which called for an end to imperialism and colonialism and rooted for the promotion of industrialisation as the legitimate way for development for the newly independent countries.

While Mkandawire has made considerable efforts to outline the process of African development, it is unclear what will happen to African peasants, artisans and traders. Spatial manifestations of Africa's development consist of patchworks or islands of development spaces that are similar to those in Europe and North America (as can be seen at Gigiri and Westlands in Nairobi) but majority of the people are engaged in widespread and large economic informality as traders, artisans or as small-scale peasant and artisanal fisherfolk.

South African anthropologist Mafeje (1981) argues the case for an indigenous development. According to Adesina (2008), Mafeje challenged African scholarship on tribes' political economy and social formation and argued that African scholarship should be rooted in indigeneity. Mafeje argues that tribal land was never a 'communal' property. In the 1990s, when the debate of land tenure and rights was propounded as the obstacle to the development of African agriculture in the continent, Mafeje (1991) observed the following:

> Traditional African community did not conceive of land in terms of ownership but in terms of dominium eminens within which use-rights were guaranteed. These were activated through family units and could get entrenched, depending on demographic pressure and the use to which different types of soil were put. The fact that individual families were units of production as well as of appropriation and could hold their plots of land in perpetuity as long as they were underuse casts doubt on the supposition by liberal economists and Marxists alike that the so-called communal land tenure necessarily militated against the development material forces in Africa. It is important to note that capitalist production has occurred in black Africa since the introduction of cash crops, without any significant changes in land tenure systems but more in land use. We are also reminded of the fact that in the Orient production increased and great technological innovations occurred over a very long time, without the development

of individual property rights. The same is true of the great, pre-Columbian empires of Latin America. In the light of all this, individual property rights, as necessary condition for development, must remain an attribute of European natural theology. (Mafeje 1991: 109)

While Lewis (1954) and Hart (1973) attempted to explain the positioning of African traditional economies *vis a vis* the modern economy, Mafeje responded with a 1978 paper titled: *Beyond 'Dual Theories' of Economic Growth*. In this paper, he argues that the traditional economy is closely linked to the modern economy in cities. It does not exist as an isolated phenomenon in the space economy of African countries.

He tried to address the half-truths and misconceptions surrounding the positioning of African peasants in the global economy that may have influenced the choice of the development models applied. It is regrettable that his works are not given space in much of the development studies literature on the state of African peasants, artisans and traders. According to Mafeje, there is need to study peasant, artisan and trader communities, especially their logic of indigenous production and exchange, transaction strategies, ideologies as well as their understanding of wellbeing and wealth. This will help the development community to engage with the structural transformation of peasants, artisans and traders.

Apart from development scholars trying to come up with strategies for development, African governments have attempted to do the same. The Kenya government has a blueprint referred to as Kenya: Vision 2030 (GoK, 2007). The blueprint advocates for massive infrastructure to replace the old colonial and dilapidated infrastructure. The new infrastructure includes Standard Gauge railway lines, new ports, special economic zones, superhighways and large scale projects such as the Lamu Port-South Sudan-Ethiopia-Transport (LAPSSET) in the frontier districts.

Urbanisation forms the spatial configuration of modern capitalist societies. Increased urbanisation is envisioned to remove people from village entrappings and take them to cities in economies of agglomeration as both labour and markets. In spite of this perspective, most production and exchange in Africa still takes place in the informal sector involving peasants, traders and artisans (Stuart, Samman and Hunt, 2018).

In Nairobi, for example, most of the jobs created in the city are from the informal sector. Due to the organic dynamism between peasants, artisans and traders, the vanquishing of the village has not taken place. They have evolved a new phenomenon, the 'African metropolis' (Kinyanjui 2016) which imparts indigeneous logic and norms of production and exchange and surplus disposal in the city. The sprawling African metropolis is best described as unplanned or informal in the post colony.

Critics of Africa's Capitalist development like Guy Mhone (2000) argue that the results of grand development projects and elite-led development have elicited patchworks of development. Guy Mhone refers to this form of phenomenon as enclave development. The rest of the development space is populated with people engaged in economic informality as traders and artisans or as small-scale peasants or artisanal fisherfolk. Their surplus is saved and circulated in friends and community Sacco's locally referred to as *chama*, rather than in banks.

The Chinese model of integrating Africa into the global economy involves working with governments and the elite in infrastructure development and manufacturing. Through its FOCAC meetings, China has convinced African leaders that it has mutual interest with Africa. In the FOCAC meeting in South Africa in 2015, the Chinese government offered to embark on an industrialisation policy that will see the country's excess capacity industries located in African countries. The costs of these investments to future generations are neither quantified nor considered.

Africa has also failed to learn from the economic history of colonisation, import substitution policy and, more recently, liberalisation and export processing. Most times, the industrialisation policy does not take into consideration the displacement and dislocation of the African input that has already been expended in development such as women peasants, artisan and traders' production and exchange.

Proposals have been made to restore the global capitalist development. Some of the scholars who have made the proposals to restructure global development include Keith Hart (1973) and David Harvey (2014). Hart (1973) calls for the evolution of a human economy that is centred on people, reproduces human life, appreciates variety in human life and values solidarity. Such an economy yields unity of self with the society. It recognises that while the market economy is legitimate, a market that knows no limits poses a threat to democracy. He questions whether capitalist markets should be the main strategy for organising the economy.

Harvey (2014) advocates for revolutionary humanism as the solution to the current global capitalism crisis. Revolutionary humanism entails an anti-capitalist stance to counter the oligarchic capitalist class. Based on Harvey's proposition, there is a need to interrogate the global economy in the eyes of women peasants, artisans and traders. What drives these women? What can we draw from their efforts to construct and manage their economic activities for the global economy amidst what Harvey (2014) terms as seventeen contradictions of capital? Can women peasants, traders and artisans be part of the architects of the restructuring of the global economy? How do women peasants, artisans and traders fit in the architecture of the new global economy? What means should be used to incorporate them in these models of the global economy?

Resistance and Resilience to Global Development

Communities respond to global capitalist development with resistance and resilience in equal measure. Communities do not want their surplus to be appropriated by the state. Communities form strategic alliances with others in different geographic places and classes. For example, during the Mau Mau peasant struggle, the educated elite were co-opted into their struggle. However, following independence, the elites embarked on a catch-up development paradigm through capitalist firms instead of facilitating the self-reliance and the solidarity of the peasants, traders and artisans. The elite hijacked the development agenda and focused on helping themselves rather than enhancing peasant production. The government elite legitimised their participation in business in the Ndegwa Commision of 1969. The commission allowed civil servants to own businesses. Many civil servants started running businesses as they worked in government.

Below are reports from the dailies of peasants and traders' resistance to what they regard as repressive regulations and penalties. Today, devolved county governments experience a lot of resistance when they want to impose levies on peasants, artisans and traders.

> Traders at the modern Taveta market near the border with Tanzania have complained of double taxation from both the Kenyan and Tanzanian authorities. They claim that they are charged by the Tanzanian immigration officials when bringing produce from the nearby towns in the country. They also claim that they are also

charged for the same when they cross over to Kenya. Besides, when they get into Taita Taveta County, they are made to pay levies as well (Mnyamwenzi, 2017).

Fresh produce traders in Nairobi have welcomed a declaration that new taxes imposed by county governments are illegal. Speaking to the Daily Nation on Wednesday morning, the chairman of the All Wakulima Traders Association, Mr Syrus Kaguta, said that the declaration came as a relief for traders and farmers using Nairobi's County-run fresh produce markets. "We are glad that the Senate has recognised that governors are not involving all stakeholders in making their decisions. We were also not consulted. We now want the higher fees removed," he said. The National Treasury Principal Secretary, Mr Kamau Thugge had earlier told the Senate's Finance Committee that new taxes imposed by county governments were illegal. Governors, he said, had failed to consult the National Government before imposing the levies. These sentiments were echoed by the senators, who called for the suspension of the new taxes. Last year, the Nairobi City County introduced a raft of new levies. Some of the fee increments would have seen traders operating in the markets pay up to 50 per cent more for services. Wakulima Market, also known as Marikiti, is Nairobi's largest fresh produce market. Traders from the market had taken to the streets protesting the new fees.

Nairobi City County governor, Dr Evans Kidero, told reporters that his government was set to implement the new market fees despite protests by traders. However, the move by senators and the Treasury to declare the taxes illegal is likely to throw these plans awry. Mr Thugge yesterday warned that new levies and rate increments introduced by the counties have the potential to harm the business climate in Kenya, thereby adversely affecting the country's economic growth prospects. Kenya slipped seven positions to be ranked 122 out of 189 countries in the World Bank's 2014 Ease of Doing Business report. The country scored worst in the "Paying Taxes" category where it was ranked 166 out of 189 countries surveyed. Traders from Marikiti also accuse the county government of failing to carry out consultations in a new plan to relocate the market to Eastlands. On Monday, Dr Kidero said that Wakulima Market will be moved to a new facility set to be constructed on Outer Ring Road. "We do not doubt the intentions to decongest the city but the County government needs to speak to the businessmen about such big decisions," said Mr Kaguta (Daily Nation, 2014)

Reports in the press recently stated that under the Busia County Finance Bill, locals would be asked to pay Kshs 700 as maternity fees,

Kshs 50 for each chicken and duck reared; and Kshs 1,000 per dog kept at home per year. A further 'dog licence fee' was set at Kshs 2,000, with cows being charged at Kshs 500 per cow, and sheep, goats and pigs being charged at Kshs 200 each. The charge for parking a trailer was set at Kshs 500." (Busia County Government, 2013)

This resistance suggests that peasants, artisans and traders have consciousness and ideological positions that influence their economic and political actions. They have logic, norms and values that guide their resistance. The resistance is not spontaneous but planned. This calls for the need for creativity in coming up with new strategies for global development that incorporates Wanjiku's creativity, resilience and institutions.

Towards a Strategy for Global Development

The survival of peasants, artisans and traders in the global economy is surrounded by many challenges arising from academic discourse, development planners and power elite. Academic and development discourse categorises them under the rubric of the informal sector and labels them using such terms as conservative, traditional, primitive, backward, unsophisticated, traditional, docile, uncultured, unregulated, criminal and stunted survivalists. However, women peasants, artisans and traders' survival into the 21st Century Africa cannot be taken for granted especially when corporate capitalism is experiencing multiple crises and relying heavily on government bailouts.

Rather than seeing their survival into the 21st Century from Polanyi's (1994) view as resistance towards the infiltration of money and self-regulating market, academia, development planners and power elite have adopted a condescending perspective towards them and calls for their modernisation and liberalisation. The discourse ignores the peasants' agency, resilience and insurgency in production and exchange or their struggle or realising wellbeing and wealth.

Early commentators on peasant, artisan and trader transformation such as Lewis (1954) recommended that their manner of operation should be first destroyed and then transformed. He recommended the development of a modern enclave, which comprised large-scale manufacturing and agriculture as the solution for development. He perceived the traditional sector to be largely unproductive and unsuitable for development catch-up. Scholars like (Koffi, 1977), however, differed with the Lewis' (1954) stance. After demonstrating how efforts to transform peasants such as the Azande in South Sudan and South African peasant labour migration had failed, he proposed the use of populist methodologies like the Maoist strategies applied in China. The Chinese transformation embraced the coexistence of small and large industries.

The postcolonial theory and development studies do not clearly outline what the peasants' colonial resistance was. They focus on the elite side of the resistance whose interest was to take over from colonial rulers without transforming the colonial structures of domination, control and exploitation. The peasants' resistance movements demanded overall transformation of domination, control and exploitation of colonial structures. They were concerned about liberation of their modes of production.

Development academic scholars were fixated on extending global capitalism through catch-up policies. They failed to come up with policies that would tap on the creativity, resilience of ordinary people. They did not initiate an economic dialogue between African modes of production and society organisation with western one. Their endeavour was to destroy and replace the mode of production of peasants, artisans and traders with the western mode of self-regulating markets and evolution of fictitious commodities of money, land and labour. They encouraged the opening up of markets consequently killing domestic production. Unlike postcolonial literary and cultural theorists who have come up with other forms of literature and art such as hip hop, orature and African art, development scholars have failed to initiate economic production and philosophies illuminated by African philosophies of accumulation, production, exchange and wellbeing.

Foreign direct investments and foreign aid are therefore proposed as the palliative solutions for lifting African economies. The strategies proposed have encouraged capital flight and left Africa heavily indebted. For example, Ndikumana and Boyce (2018) observe that between 1970-2015, thirty African countries lost a combined $1.4 trillion through capital flight over a 46-year period. Interest earnings on capital flight brought the cumulative amount to $1.8 trillion, an amount that greatly surpassed the stock of debt owed by these countries as of 2015 ($496.9 billion). This development made the countries "net creditors" to the rest of the world.

Moreover, The countries lost more through capital flight than they received in the form of aid or foreign private investment. There is little understanding of the *raison d'étre* of peasant, artisan and trade activities and their survival into the 21st Century. For this structural transformation to happen, there is a need to understand why past efforts did not succeed and what the peasants have been doing while the rest of the world was transforming. The structural transformation of peasant production is slow primarily because there are limited attempts to explain the raison d'être of peasant economies, logic of production and understanding of wealth and wellbeing. This is because the sociological and anthropological analysis of peasant, artisan and trader communities is limited. Most of the commissioned studies investigate problems and challenges, perceptions, lack of productivity, lack of income, lack of education, lack of technology, lack of incentives, and lack of policies. They attempt to attribute causality to factors that may not necessarily be the ones responsible for peasant activities. The analysis assumes that there is a universal economic model, which peasants, artisans and traders should adopt so that they may transform.

This author sees the transformation taking place in the context of *utu-ubuntu* through the action of traders, artisans and smallholder farmers and fisher folk. As Bishop Desmond Tutu (1999) aptly observes, embracing *ubuntu* will spur sustainability and resilience in our global economy. This wouldl involve using resources for the welfare of the other persons, collective action, solidarity and sharing. The marketplace is viewed as a nest where individuals nurture themselves in livelihood negotiation and perform solidarity entrepreneurialism in order to fulfill life goals and obligations.

The critique of development studies is provided in this book by the analysis of Wanjiku in global development. Wanjiku's experience in production and exchange is the embodiment of real development among people who contribute to development through their everyday livelihood struggle for survival. They feed cities with grains, vegetables, meat and fish. They supply products like coffee and tea to global multinationals. They struggle with everyday issues of exploitation by global and local capitalism in the name of development. With their resilience they struggle to articulate their indigeneity and gender difference in production and exchange.

CHAPTER THREE

WANJIKU IN GLOBAL DEVELOPMENT

During the clamour for Kenya's multiparty democracy in the 1990s, a seniour citizen stood out in the procession of those seeking reforms. In her raised hands was a placard that advocated for democracy. Her move was daring since pro-multiparty rallies were often met with violent police brutality. The woman was christened 'Wanjiku' to represent ordinary Kenyan citizens who stood their ground to agitate for wider democratic space. Wanjiku is the low income earner, peasant, petty commodity producer, trader, farmer, fishmonger and artisan. She does not belong to the elite class. She has moderate education and representation of the proletariat, indigeneity and the interests of the non-elite in Kenya's politics of global development.

In spite of her lowly position in society, Wanjiku is linked to the global economy through her everyday livelihood negotiation. She produces and sells the food that feeds workers in multinational and government corporations in cities. She produces commodities such as tea, coffee, sugarcane and cotton for multinational global value chains. Wanjiku is disadvantaged and marginalised in global development despite her hard work. Her marginalisation dates from the colonial period to the postcolonial state. Through her logic and solidarity, Wanjiku has been resilient in adapting and resisting modernity and global capitalism by maintaining an economic model that caters for her household and community. While global development is based on a patriarchal capitalist model, Wanjiku offers an alternative feminine economic model. Through this model, she has played a critical role in connecting people through space and time and creating flourishing households and communities.

In global development, Wanjiku is part of the large scale peasant and petty commodity production and exchange in Africa. African peasants are small-scale agriculture producers occupying their own land or squatting on other peoples' land. They produce both for subsistence and selling. Most of the food consumed in the cities and urban centres as well as foodstuff meant for export such as coffee, tea, cocoa, avocadoes, fruits and bananas is produced by them. They also keep animals such as cows and goats and rear chicken. The term 'peasant' in this book includes artisans and traders because they rely on their own labour and resources. Artisans engage in the production of tools and implements while traders move food commodities between the farmers and the consumers. Wanjiku is part of this closely interlinked peasant and petty production or 'indigene economies' which have survived colonialism, modernisation and market liberalisation.

Wanjiku is both a class economic category and political society which acts as a movement for both transformation and indigenisation. These twin roles have made it difficult to understand Wanjiku, an embodiment of the global and local visceral effects of global capitalism. She demonstrates why we always have coffee in world capitals while coffee farmers remain poor. She also explains why there is a lot of food in urban households and restaurants yet farmers are poor.

Incorporating Wanjiku into Global Development

In Kenya, Wanjiku produces most of the food and agricultural exports except flowers; manufactures of household goods such as construction material, furniture, school uniforms, water gutters and farm implements. Wanjiku also plays a vital role in the distribution of goods and services. Wanjiku operates in rural areas and marginal spaces in cities and towns which are characterised by neglect in terms of infrastructure. She is often viewed as unsophisticated, traditional, docile and uncultured. Although Nyeko (2014) describes traders as dirty, frustrated and devoid of moral decorum, they provide essential services to labourers in the industrial area and markets around the estates. Understanding why they still thrive in the 21st Century Africa global development is a key question that development practise must address in order to evolve a global economy that is inclusive and sustainable.

An economic base determines everything else in society. A capitalist economic system will have a capitalist state, law that upholds capitalist economic relations and a government that reflects the economic interests of the dominant class. Cultural production and education institutions will be structured to reinforce the economic system. Society is built on an economic foundation and the means of relation of production in this foundation will bring about the characteristics of other segments of society. The current global capitalist economic system has a patriarchal face hinged on the philosophy of the 'rational economic man'. The rational economic man is a risk taker, an innovator, aggressive, creative, fact driven and engages in transactions that are valued monetarily.

From a Marxist perspective, global development is capitalist. The development of capitalism takes place when peasants are transformed into wage labourers and are divorced from subsistence production. They are removed from the soil to work for merchant and industrial capitalists.

Wanjiku's experience, however, has been different. She has not abandoned her mode of production in exchange for working for merchants and industrialists in the labour market. She still trades, works on the farm, or makes her products. Her production is centred in the household and community. Viewed from a Marxist feminist lens, Wanjiku's reproduction activities, economic production and exchange take place in a non-market situation that is not reckoned in government statistics. Wanjiku's activities are therefore unplanned for or unpaid for.

While elite women workers may pursue liberation and demand for paid maternity leave, reduction of working hours, decent working spaces or equality in leadership positions in corporations and government boardrooms, Wanjiku does not ask for these facilities because she works for herself in the household and community. That said, Wanjiku's interlocked private and public spheres expose her to exclusion and exploitation. It is in this space that Wanjiku has centred her sociality, production, exchange, logic and solidarities in livelihood negotiation. She has created her own savings groups (*chama*) where money is held communally and shared among members (Podlashuc, 2009, Kinyanjui 2012; Caretta and Cheptuma, 2019).

Towards an Analytical Frame for Positioning Wanjiku in Global Development

The existence of Wanjiku may be viewed within the decolonial feminist lens (Lugones, 2010). Lugones observes that colonised people were viewed as non-human, satanic, infantile, aggressively sexual and in need of civilisation through incorporation into capitalist production and Western bourgeois modernity. Colonised women were placed in the lowest rung of the human civilisation ladder. Oyeronke (1997) observes that 'woman' is an invention of Western discourses. Colonialism created a racialized and capitalist coloniality of gender characterised by gender oppression. In Kenya, people who adopted Western modernity were initially referred to as the *mambere* (the pioneers) or *athomi* (the educated). Today, these groups and their descendants form the rising middle class. This rising middle class has imbued and is characterised by capitalism, western modernity culture and consumption habits and modes of production. They continue the role of colonising, civilising and spreading of capitalist ideas to the rest. Wanjiku, the ordinary citizen, is outside the middle-class circle and derives livelihood in peasant production, artisanry and trade.

In Western epistemology, Wanjiku's economy is referred to as peasant, petty commodity or informal sector. Some economic, sociology and anthropology frameworks were racialised and geared to reproduce or observe colonial difference. The evidence of racialised non-human is reflected in the terminologies such as 'survivalist,' 'subsistence,' 'disorganised' and 'criminal' when referring to the informal sector. The terms resonate with the colonial mentality that the African is less human and is incapable of coming up with development and economic models that can be compared with Western capitalism.

It is not clear why for example, Hart (1971, 1973) and ILO (1972) used the term informal sector to describe an African indigenous method of doing business. According to ILO (1972) Report on Employment, Incomes and Inequality in Kenya, the informal sector has the characteristics shown in Table 2.

Table 2: Characteristics of Informal and Formal Sectors

Informal	Formal
Ease of entry	Difficult of entry
Reliance on indigenous resources	Frequent reliance on overseas resources
Family ownership	Corporate ownership
Small scale of operation	Large scale of operation
Labour intensive and adapted technologies	Capital intensive and often imported technologies
Skills acquired outside formal school system	Formally acquired skills, often expatriate
Unregulated and competitive markets	Protected markets (through tariffs, quota and trade license)

Source:ILO, 1972: 6)

A critical look at the seven attributes of the informal sector reveals that, as defined by Hart (1971, 1973) and ILO (1972), it was an indigenous economic model which is open, inclusive, independent and creative like any other. It is geared towards surplus that supports flourishing families and communities. The attribute, *ease of entry*, is a strong point in terms of inclusivity while *reliance on indigenous resources* is a way of saving foreign exchange. *Family ownership* is a method of inclusion and redistribution within the household that ensures transfer of skill and resources to the next generation. *Small scale of operation* may denote that small is beautiful and it could eschew all the benefits of small scale of operation. *Skill acquisition outside formal schooling* means that every individual including those rejected by the elitist formal schooling system can join in the sector. *Unregulated competitive markets* mean that every individual has the chance to participate in the market without restriction.

It appears that the so-called informal economy was an invention of the Western anthropological and sociological epistemology to describe an indigenous economic phenomenon consisting of peasants, artisans and traders. This phenomenon was open, inclusive, labour intensive, competitive and creative in terms of adapting technology attributes as well strategic in saving foreign exchange. It was imbued with the principles of self-rule, self-reliance, sharing, gifting and reciprocity. This means that if embraced, it could help solve some of the problems that the postcolonial states experience. Unfortunately, the postcolonial states through development aid, local and foreign experts have advocated for the formalisation of this sector. Formalisation creates difficulty of entry, forces reliance on foreign technology, entrenches corporate ownership, requires capital intensiveness, and imposes reliance on expatriates, use of imported technology and protection of markets. Without a doubt, the costs of formalisation have been high and time-wasting.

Economic and sociological coloniality for women entails financial inclusion into global financial circuits and architecture. This has created problems such as indebtedness, depeasantisation, joblessness, neoliberal patriarchy, loss of control of household production, lack of peace and harmony in the family and community, impoverishment, and exploitation by both local and global merchants.

These are challenges that Wanjiku contends with in her everyday livelihood negotiation for survival. Wanjiku's multifaceted reaction to these challenges using ways such as resistance, resilience and indigenisation has made her mode of production and exchange to survive into the 21ˢᵗ Century. It is for this reason that scholars, policy makers and development experts need to learn from the women peasants, artisans and traders in order to understand their logic, norms, values and institutions in their livelihood negotiations within the context of economic and sociological coloniality.

Wanjiku's decolonial perspective is expressed in one of the Nyakinyua (senior women group) songs. After independence, Nyakinyua women celebrated the fact that freedom had given them the ability to grow crops. As a result of this, they were able to nurture their children. In one of their songs, they say that: *Rĩrĩa Kenyatta arĩ Lodwar ĩĩ ciana citũ cia rĩaga managu. Na rĩrĩa okire, Ngĩ handa mbembe, Ngĩ handa njahĩ na ngirĩndi ya gukama iria.* (When Kenyatta was jailed in Lodwar, we used to feed our children on wild vegetables, but when he was freed, we are able to plant beans, maize and own grade cattle that give us milk). This consciousness of nurturing influences Wanjiku's acts of insurgency, collaboration, joy and despondency in production and exchange.

In this song, Wanjiku expresses the expectations and demands that she wanted met by the independent government. Of course, times and situations have changed, and the above song for asking the state to give them goodies has been replaced by Constituency Development Fund (CDF) grant proposals. There is also emphasis on public participation in the dialogue and design of projects through town-hall meetings. It is also politically correct in development and political language to speak about acting and representing Wanjiku - the face of peasants in Kenya. But there is increasing evidence that most women do not attend such meetings. One Kenyan local daily on Afrobarometer results noted that women are less likely than men to discuss politics, contact political leaders, join activist groups and attend community meetings.

Wanjiku enters global development with a logic of nurturing and building solidarities. Much of the literature on Wanjiku's participation in global development provides information on the hurdles that she encounters. These include: patriarchal land rights that accord land to men; juggling her limited time with domestic responsibilities of reproduction; technology disadvantage (Henn 1983); biased customary laws and agricultural policies that reward men rather than women (Boserup, 1970). Faced with these challenges, Wanjiku does not give up. She negotiates her livelihood with determination and resilience. Perhaps, it is due to her desire for a revolutionary change that will centre her logic, sociality, production and exchange, cultural and intergenerational transfer and exchange of life that she joins other demonstrators on street protests.

Current thinkers (Federici, 2012, Vakkyil 2017) on former colonised groups or indigenous communities have observed that indigenity is articulated to global development while women tend to maintain their gender difference. By articulating indigeneity, communities construct their identity and meaning to their everyday practices. Federici (2012) observes that women create their own commons while Vakkyil (2017) argues that they integrate by introducing the characteristics of their indigenous businesses such as collective-owned and managed businesses, reciprocity, trust and promotion of socio-cultural practises in the business. Essentially, they aim at domesticating capitalism. This analysis helps us raise these questions: How does Wanjiku articulate indigeneity and gender difference in her daily life? What economic models does she create or craft in order to advance her livelihood and survival?

Articulating Wanjiku in Global Development from Above

The African male was the first to be introduced into the global capitalist economy as a worker in mines and plantations or a domestic servants. He was the first to have money for use in production, exchange and consumption. His monetisation was not a smooth one. He would be arrested for lack of money in his pocket or failure to pay tax. He was thus forced to take up jobs in factories, mines and plantations. Men who had no jobs entered the global circuits of money by selling goats, sugarcane, honey and tobacco. Women entered the global circuits of money by trading in products like yams, bananas, beans, sweet potatoes and grains.(Kinyanjui, 2015; Fibaek and Green, 2019)

In Kenya, the 1928 Metropolitan Ordinance was the first real attempt to plan for global development through urbanisation and monetisation in the colonial period. It laid down rules and regulations on property rights and occupier premises. It also outlined the rules of governing the city by determining the constitution of the council. It defined the participation of different communities in the urban economy through zoning. It provided for the layout of the native locations, land, housing and industrial sites. Africans' participation in the colonial economy was through street trading or hawking. Trade was guided by regulations which defined offensive trades, situation of food and drink, peddlers and hawkers, markets, native labour, native locations, native passes and licencing. The ordinance positioned the African male in the city and regulated his nature of businesses and manner of conducting business.

African participation in the economy was also regulated through licencing and payment of market dues. The licencing was not automatic. It was subject to approval by a committee. Business Licencing was for an individual, not family. This was contrary to the spirit and ethos of the African markets which were free and open to all. The ordinance gave the African limited access to global capital markets. African traders and artisans were referred to as 'hawkers'. According to Bylaw 325 of the 1928 Metropolitan Ordinance, a hawker was defined as '...*any person who whether as principal, agent, employee carries on the business of offering or exposing goods for sale, barter or exchange, elsewhere than at a fixed place'*. The hawker was mainly an African male.

Urbanisation and monetisation spelt out in the 1928 Metropolitan Act were integral to the incorporation of Africans to the capitalist global economy development. However, like wage employment, it initiated the African male into the global capitalist economy. Thus, the metropolitan ordinance excluded the participation of women in the global economy and financial circuits.

To articulate Wanjiku in the global economy, the World Bank and the United Nations have come up with women empowerment programmes. There are many gains associated with women empowerment. They include the ability of women to put food on the table for their familities, reduction of women's dependency on their male partners for money as well as independence and dignity for women. Women, like their male counterparts, are able to make monetary transactions in production, exchange and consumption.

The incorporation of Wanjiku into the global economic development entails adopting the culture of money and self-regulating markets, introduction of new crops to replace indigenous ones, introduction of new technologies, changing indigenous methods of organising production and exchange and changing methods of harnessing human agency.

Wanjiku has resisted some of these things. Women economic empowerment models have been promoted within the heavily masculine patriarchal capitalist economic system, leaving women with little room to create their own economic models that are based on affection, solidarity, gifting, sharing and reciprocity.

Despite the fact that peasant women have been introduced to the global market system, they are still invisible and disenfranchised in global consumption outlets. They have very little share of the global wealth generated from the sale of commodities. The women's footprints are not reflected in packages of products such as coffee, tea, cocoa, flowers, fish, vegetables, bead work, or craft's in industries, supermarkets, homes, schools and offices. Global merchant industrialists who add value to peasants, artisans and traders commodities do not also acknowledge them. Thus, the ownership of the manufactured products is transferred from the women to the industrialists and global merchants.

Wanjiku's Attempts to Articulate into the Global Economy

Although women were not integrated into the global economy, they joined it through trade in commodities like beans (Claire Robertson, 1997) or through prostitution (White, 1980). The growing urban population needed food while the large male population who had left their wives in rural areas needed sex. According to Robertson (1997), Gikuyu and Kamba women found their way into the global capitalist economy through their female genius of collective strength.

> "Here we see the fundamental importance of women's work in creating a new world, but also how they overcame difficulties by using collective strength predicated upon the old world and delineated by the objectification imposed upon women by colonialism to mediate and transform the new situation. In so doing women offered a reconstruction of gender that has transformative value for the society. Contravening the stereotype of East African women as docile farmers, this history explores the symmetry of symbolic and material categories in making beans and other dried staples the focus of a commodity-based history of trade that foregrounds the submerged voices of those whom colonialists and tourists found/find invisible. If they were noticed, they were not wanted, like the beans in the maize fields of colonial agriculture officers promoting maize monoculture. Robertson, (1997: 2)."

The women, pushed by trouble, their resilience and the need to nurture their families joined the global economy and financial circuits. They did not do this as the 'rational economic man.' The women grow grains, legumes, vegetables and tubers. They also grow cash crops such as coffee, cocoa, tea, pyrethrum, spices and flowers. They take care of animals like cows and goats and chicken. They produce craft products such as pottery, craft, garments, implements, beadworks, leather, toys and ornaments.

Wanjiku is a remnant of traditional African societies before colonialism, modernisation and market liberalisation. She has been a resistor and resilient adopter. She articulates her peasant indigeneity and gender difference to global development. As a resistor, she has stuck to her peasant mode of production and exchange which is often construed as an indicator of the failure of the development project in African countries. She has maintained traditional skills of crafting and management. Her peasant indigeneity is articulated to global development by her ability to maintain the sharing, solidarity, reciprocity, small scale production, self-sufficiency, self-reliance and self-determination in production and exchange. As a resilient adopter of global development, she has monetised her household production and exchange strategically. She has also included education and meeting the healthcare needs of her offspring and parents as part of her consumption, production and reproduction. She has maintained her gender difference in her nurturing and caring logic in production and exchange.

Wanjiku also maintains her gender difference in the economic arena through solidarities and locating capital in family accounts and SACCOs; or with the local social welfare group called *chama*. Kinship and neighbourliness determine economic transactions in the household or family economy. Economic transactions are supported by a series of social transactions that include solidarity, gifting and reciprocity. Wanjiku works on land and uses her own labour and resources to manage her firms and businesses. Global development necessitates the need to initiate innovations for structural transformation of this form of economic model.

CHAPTER FOUR

WANJIKU'S RESISTANCE, TRAUMA AND TRANSFORMATION

To understand Wanjiku's 21st Century worldview, it is important to interrogate the resistance, trauma and transformation occasioned by the processes of violence, dispossession, exclusion and isolation by postcolonial capitalism and modernity processes. My journal entry of my day in Uthiru reflects, to a large extent, resistance to modernity in Dagoretti, Nairobi.

14th February, 2015.

> I am seated at Uthiru. The compounds have a mixture of stone and *mabati* (corrugated iron sheet) buildings. There is no evidence of landscaping. Stone buildings with toilets on the outside and indigenous trees such as *mukinduri*, and *mugumo miiri* dot the compound. I can see brightly coloured kiosks and faded *mabati* roofs. The house walls are mostly black and brown and one can't tell when they last received a coat of paint. Women adorn ordinary *mabiriri* dresses and head scarfs. Typical of rural settings, the roads and pavements have accumulated dust from the prevailing lateritic soil as all humus has been eroded. Gullies of various depths dot the roadside. Some men are selling water from a *mkokoteni* (pushcart) while others are just idling. A *mugumo* tree towers above the nearby buildings. The compound owner tells me that he is going to get rid of buildings encroaching on the *mugumo* tree. Traders and artisans carry out their exchange of goods and services on the road side. Some sell bananas, while others sell maize and other sell withered grocery. The latter is a sign that the weather has been bad. Some women wash clothes from a common tap and hang them on a line to dry. To access the city centre from Uthiru, one has to part with at least 50 Kenya Shillings.

8th October, 2016.

> I am attending my cousin's *ngurario* ceremony (the final ceremony to celebrate a Gikuyu wedding after bride price has been paid). The bridegroom works in the tech industry and has brought his co-workers to witness the ceremony. He belongs to the third generation in the family to embrace Christianity. The girl and the boy's parents have contributed greatly towards the cost of the celebration. The ceremony

is the ultimate gift to the bride and groom by their parents, family and friends.

The key aspect of the ceremony is the *gutinia kiande* that involves the bridegroom symbolically cutting a goat's shoulder plate to symbolise sharing and leaning on each other. The man shares the different parts of meat which symbolise sexuality, reproduction and production. The woman in turn gives the husband cooked porridge. The ceremony is accompanied by gifting and celebration.

Guests are taken through a lecture on decolonising the family and marriage ceremonies. We are informed that missionaries and colonialists labelled most traditional African practices as pagan.

What does the ceremony tell about the wellbeing of the family and community? Which school did the groom, who was well-versed with the bible and modern technology celebrant, go to seeing that he embraced the traditional ceremony which missionaries condemned? The ceremony is clearly part of the resistance to the capitalist and modernity project. It is a triple process that encompasses resistance, trauma and transformation of postcolonial societies.

20th December, 2016.

Citizen TV airs a live broadcast of a Luo cultural ceremony in Homa Bay. The ceremony has brought together four counties of Luo Nyanza and attracted the political class, professionals, women, youth, and the Luo council of elders. The ceremony features traditional Luo regalia, brews, food, artefacts and dances. The climax of the ceremony is the initiation of Joseph Nanok, the Governor from the far-flung Turkana County, in recognition of his effort to champion for the Turkana culture. He is given a traditional Luo cap, bag, shield and spear, all symbols of authority among the Luo. In his acceptance speech, he beseeches all Luo-speaking people from around the world to embrace their culture and remind themselves of where they came from. A proposal is also made to start a cultural institute that would advance and protect the Luo Culture as a springboard for unifying people through culture.

While engaging in the economy and its activities, Wanjiku resists practices she considers to be detrimental to her culture. She resists through the oral word that is passed on through families in chats, narratives or songs. She is influenced by the fear of losing control of what she already has, or losing identity as a family, community or society. She adopts principles and tenets of capitalist production and modernity that are in harmony with their cultural practices, hence

42

the preservation of cultural commodity production activities such as artisanal fisherfolk and peasantry. The Luo cultural ceremony, for example, gave peasants, artisans and traders an opportunity to display their artefacts, regalia, pottery, traditional foods and brews.

One of the earliest form of resistance towards capitalist production and exchange, well-being and wealth in the Kenyan context is expressed in one of my paternal grandmother's favourite song, *Mbia Ciokire* (when money was introduced):

Mbia ciokire ikerehe ūthu na rūmena	With money came enmity and contempt
Mūndū arandūrage nyina	A person demands back money she readily gave to her mother
Ūria ūngī arandūrage mūka rīria me toro	A man is asking his wife for money as they lie in bed
Ūui mbia ciokire	Oh, what money came to do!
*Ngucu ni ngucucu iiyo *2*	A jackal is a skinny cow *2
Ngūkama ngarūthi na ndiume iria	I go to milk my Ngaruthi, I get not a drop
Mbia ciokire	Oh, what money came to do!
*Nī ngūūria kiūria *2*	I ask you a question *2
Wī kanyoni mūthemba ū?	What kind of bird are you?
Ūi mbia ciokire	Oh, what money came to do!
Nī ngūkūūria kīngī	I ask you another question
Nyūkwa mathiaga na ū?	Whose company does your mother keep?
Mbia ciokire	Oh, what money came to do!
Mathiaga na kiondo na kahiu	She travels with a string bag and a knife.
Ni ngūkūūria kīngī	I ask you another question
Nyamindigi yakaga ku?	Where does the red-breasted thrush build its nest?
Yakaga kigwaini ii iyo	It builds its nest among the sugar cane
Mbia ciokire	Oh, what money brought!
*Nī ngūkwoya ngūtae ii yo*2*	I'll hoist you up and throw you *2
Ngwagararie ikūmbi rīa mūthūnū	Throw you over the granary
Mbia ciokire	Oh what money brought!
*Ngūkama Ngarūthi iiyo*2*	Milking my cow Ngaruthi
Ndakama Ndīroima iria	It is not giving milk
Mbia ciokire	Oh what money brought!

According to the song, money has alienated people from humanness and solidarity in the household economy. It has affected the relationship between husband, wife, mother and son. Humaneness and solidarity were the centres of production and exchange in African communities and served as the basis for sharing, caring, generosity and reciprocity between actors in the economy. With the advent of the money culture, *mundu arandurage nyina*: children started demanding that parents repay what they owed them. After your mother who nurtured you borrows some money from you, it is insulting to insist and demand that she repays it. You owe her a lot! *Uria ungi arandurage muka mari uriri metoro:* likewise, a husband in the intimacy of their bedroom demanding that his wife repays the money she owes him is repulsive. It affects the caring and sharing, as well as the sacrifice required in marriage. The song laments that the tools of production, *kiondo na kahiu,* or basket and knife have been rendered useless. New farm inputs which need new technologies have been introduced. Land used for cultivation has been subdivided and turned into real estate. Forest farms where individuals could lease some land for farming have been gazetted as government property. With the entry of money, there is no longer peace. *Wi wa muthemba uriku?* People have lost identity!

The persistence of orature in poking holes into the culture of money and self-regulating markets was revived during the implementation of neoliberalism.

Les Wanyika band was a popular dance group in Tanzania in the early 80s and 90s. Their song *Shilingi Yaua Tena Maua* talks about how money is lovely and fatal at the same time. The song observes that the fabric of the society has been weakened by the money culture. Individuals without money cannot be listened to in the society. Young men have to have money to win love. Money has become the key to unlock socio-political and economic doors.

Amidst the changing social order occasioned by money, Queen Jane in her songs resists the notion of accumulation at the expense of humanity and solidarity in the family and community in *Mwanake Uyu Tiga Kwiyamba*, and *Geithia Mundu Mbia Ni Ithiraga*. She stresses the importance of including everyone in monetary acquisition and giving the pursuit and possession of money a human face.

The increased sources of finance such as venture capital, microfinance, internet investments and credit schemes have been vehemently resisted through various anecdotes and narratives. Observations such as: if you fail to return the money in good time, the owners will come for your property or demand that you sacrifice your beloved son or daughter, prevail. Examples are given of individuals who have sacrificed their sons in order to become rich. A rich home mate narrates that once, when she was sweeping her yard, one boy who was playing football with his friend told him to avoid playing near the vicinity lest the ball went to her compound. The boy explained that the compound belonged to devil worshippers. The rich home mate called out to the boy and asked him how he had learnt they were devil worshippers. The boy said he had been told by the mother due to their excess riches. The anecdotes instil fear and encourage individuals to accumulate their own funds and fund their transactions rather than become indebted. Some anecdotes discourage commodifying land. They say that if one sells land that has a grave on it, the money would disappear.

Traumas

Wanjiku is subjected to deeply distressing events that cause feelings of helplessness and diminishes her sense of self-worth. She is sometimes labelled as a criminal due to the way she dresses. She is accused of loitering and forced to part with a bribe to secure her freedom or go to court and be fined under the vagrancy and loitering law. Government officials confiscate her goods and incarcerate her for selling wares on streets. Police harassment sometimes results in extra judicial killings. Her trauma is also increased by politics of exclusion and neglect and deterioration of health infrastructure. Public hospital conditions are in a deplorable state. Patients share beds and watch the extremely sick die. One person intimated told me how he hired a vehicle to take his sister in-law to Thika District Hospital. On arrival, he took her to the emergency unit but since she was not booked for that day, she was not attended to. They left frustrated and helpless.

I also remember my experience while visiting Ngorongo health unit. At times, the hospital staff would break for tea and be engrossed in idle talk for a long time while patients waited for them to return to work. I have watched relatives stammer as they talk to stone-faced health professionals.

Inheritance Crisis

Like individuals excluded by the education system, people without inheritance become vulnerable and find their way into the informal economy. Through handing down of property and skills in form of inheritance, Kenyan communities re-distributed wealth among generations. Traditionally, land and property were bequeathed to the next generation by trustees and trusteeship handed over to the next person in the lineage. The traditional inheritance structures and practices are, however, constrained in many ways and generate vulnerability for Wanjiku and subsequently, creating an inheritance crisis in the country that is reflected in the tremendous increase in the number of disputes related to land and succession between 2004 and 2007. Table 3 provides a picture of the succession and land related cases in the country.

Table 3: Succession and Land Cases Files Between 2004 and 2007

Year	Land	%change	Succession	% change
2004	604		3,944	
2005	799	24.4	3583	-10.0
2006	1439	44.4	4146	13.5
2007	1575	8.6	4044	10.2

Source: Table 15.6 Cases filed, pending and disposed of by various magistrates' courts (Kenya, 2007 Economic Survey: p 241).

The inheritance crisis is a result of demographic and legal factors as well as changes in modes of production. With regard to demographic factors, trustees are living longer. Although HIV/ Aids has supposedly lowered the life expectancy for Kenya in the new millennium to 46 years, the number of people who are in the age cohort of 50-80 years could be greater than it was in the pre-independence days (GoK, 2007)

These individuals are less likely to bequeath their property since they also need income. Further, commodity-marketing boards and cooperatives such as Coffee Board of Kenya (CBK), Kenya Planters Co-operative Union (KPCU), Kenya Tea Development Authorities (KTDA), Flower Council, Sugarcane Authority, Pyrethrum Board, Cotton and Lint Board and Cereals Boards have limited mechanisms for dealing with intergeneration transfer of shares to siblings. If land were available, each sibling would plant their own tea, sugar, cotton, pyrethrum, flowers or coffee and register with the respective boards or cooperatives. However, as shown in Table 3 above, such an option is not available. Since the farmers only have a nominal registration rather than a limited liability company, they cannot sell off their shares to their siblings. Moreover, since these do not factor in social protection and social insurance such as old age pension, unemployment, disability and medical insurance for their members, the members would also be unwilling to let go of their nominal registration without some form of income assurance.

Unfriendly Labour Practices

Labour policies are also traumatising to the class of Wanjiku. Workers' welfare in a surplus labour economy is never considered. If one does not like the employment terms offered, someone else would be available for work. In addition, the working conditions are poor. Workers put in long hours with no benefits. They are usually employed on casual basis without social insurance or healthcare benefits. As with the hiring, they are arbitrarily laid off often without notice. It is often the case that some Nairobi's Industrial Area, Ruaraka and Baba Ndogo are surrounded by slums and low-income housing. People cannot enter into regular housing contracts because their jobs are temporary and payment terms are not certain. They are always looking for ways into self-employment as peasants, artisans and traders.

Strategies like the import-substitution industrialisation and export processing have been pursued without consideration of the type of education required, health needs and protection for workers. Import substitution and export processing firms expand and wipe out the non-modern sectors of the labour market and social policies. The import substitution industrialisation strategy, implemented soon after independence, was pursued within the context of a mental picture of a labour market with characteristics such as surplus labour that was low-skilled, usually male who were rural migrant workers who would eventually retire to the rural areas. Each of these characteristics had a significant impact on the welfare of the workers.

The surplus labour strand ensured that wages were kept low. Workers were hired and fired at will and were maintained on casual basis. Workers could easily be replaced with others every fortnight. Workers with casual contracts are usually uncertain about their jobs and fear the fact that they might be declared redundant anytime.

Others may consider themselves the lucky few and may not see the need for actively being involved in trade unions. Subsequently as the industries thrive, the workers become impoverished.

This perhaps explains why hubs of import substitution industrialisation such as Thika town, and Ruaraka area in Nairobi have poor housing, educational and health facilities. In Thika, workers from the vast import substituting industries live in Kiandutu, Pilot, and Majengo while waiting for their job contracts to be regularised. The Ruaraka area has some very old import substituting industries like Allsops, Henkel Limited and Cussons Limited and new export processing industries such as Rafiki Processing and United Aryan EPZ Limited but it is ringed by the poor neighbourhoods of Kariobangi, Baba Ndogo and Mathare.

Surprisingly, Wanjiku's trauma is used in Television commercial advertising. For example, one advert of a long-lasting battery expresses its durability by depicting that it lasts as long as the security guard's lifetime. In the commercial, the battery does not expire and the security guard waits for a lifetime. The battery expires after the guard has lost teeth and has grey hair. Implicit in this advert is that once Wanjiku is condemned to being a *jua kali* worker, she will remain so for her entire lifetime.

Trauma is rife in the booming construction industry when casual labourers are exposed to poor and dangerous working conditions. For example, most of the construction workers in the building that collapsed in downtown Nairobi in January 2006 were young adults with primary level of education.

Culture & Practices of the Elite

Elite cultures such as large motorcades in funeral trails to rural areas also cause trauma to ordinary people. Urban elites descend in village funerals with large motorcades, traumatising people whose mode of mobility is mostly walking. The vehicles are a status or class symbol. The fleet of cars remind Wanjiku of a status she cannot reach. These elites also carry along bottled water and, in some cases, packed foodstuffs, undoubtedly traumatising individuals who drink water from rural water sources. Indirectly, the elite are telling Wanjiku that the water that is being consumed in rural settings is not safe for them. The bottled water infers that Wanjiku does not care about her health. This experience reminds Wanjiku of the deep valley between the elite and her. This limits her worldview of possibilities.

Earnings from Produce

Crop marketing boards and their mode of payments are traumatising. They determine pricing and when to pay. They assume that Wanjiku is ignorant and cannot reach international markets to sell her products. They bond Wanjiku in unfair trading relationships. Wanjiku is left helpless (Kinyanjui, 2015).

In the season of 2016, peasant coffee farmers from Githoeti in Gatundu North were subjected to a traumatic experience of their lifetime. Like any other season, they had tended their crop, picked and taken it to factory. The coffee was cleaned, underwent first stage processing, dried and stored. It was just waiting for sale to processors in urban centres when, one night, thieves broke into the stores and took off with the coffee. Just like that! Wanjiku lost proceeds of her hard won sweat.

It is sad that the theft of this magnitude took place unnoticed and no arrests were made. If police guard banks and other financial institutions, why can't peasant farmers' factories be protected by regular or administration police? The pain to the peasant farmers was unbearable. No media covered the issue.

Roads and Access

The deplorable road infrastructure is traumatising. One has to battle with dust, toxic fumes, and potholes. The health impact that passengers get from inhaling smoke and dust as well as the trauma they go through when heavily shaken by potholes is unimaginable. The loss that vehicle owners also go through when repairing vehicles as a result of poor roads is immense.

Some NGOs whose mission was to offer services in areas that government could not reach or was inefficient have traumatised Wanjiku when they exit following change in priority or funding. Most NGO workers have adopted lifestyles that are beyond reach of the ordinary citizen. They drive fuel guzzlers and don't use monies for intended purposes. Most of the NGO money goes to sustain the high wages and consumption lifestyles of the respective NGO workers. Some of the projects are untenable and leave target people worse off than they were.

Transformation

In the 1990s, there was a lot of development activism and advocacy in promoting an entrepreneurial culture in micro and small enterprises, most of which were operating informally. The role of government in stimulating entrepreneurship and business development, especially among micro and small enterprises was taken over by non-governmental organisations (NGOs) during the Neo-liberalism era (Mullei and Bokea 1999). Micro and small enterprises (MSEs) were perceived to be a safety net for the majority of people affected by neoliberal policies. NGOs were promoted because the government was perceived to be inefficient, aloof and out-of-touch with the people (Burbank 1994). Initiatives such as Improve Your Business, Kenya Management Assistance Programme (K-MAP), K-Rep, Small and Micro-enterprise programme (SMEP), Women's Economic Development (WEDCO), Kenya Women Finance Trust, Faulu, Gatsby Trust, World Vision, Action Aid, and Oxfam initiated programmes to support MSEs (Namusonge, 1999). They carried out training programmes in business development services and provided credit. Most of them were largely funded by the Department for International Development (DFID) (Namusonge 1999), the United States Agency for International Development (USAID), the United Nations Development programme (UNDP), Danish International Development Agency (DANIDA), and the Swedish International Development Cooperation Agency (SIDA).

NGOs were instrumental in the passing of the Micro and Small Enterprises Act (2012). The joint effort of K-Rep bank, Central Bureau of Statistics (CBS) and International Centre for Economic Growth highlight the status of MSEs through periodic baseline surveys of MSEs. The Institute for Development Studies of the University of Nairobi and the Centre for Development Research (CDR) in Copenhagen, with support from DANIDA, produced two books that popularised MSEs which went a long way to influence policy. NGOs were actively involved in the review of business licensing that saw the introduction of the Single Business Permit.

All these efforts, notwithstanding, economic informality continues to persist in Kenyan cities, despite interventions in business development services or micro finance.

In the new millennium, the Kenyan government adopted a two-pronged strategy to promote business. The first is Kenya's Vision 2030 and the targeting of marginalised groups. Kenya's Vision 2030 aims at making the country a middle-income country by the year 2030 (Kenya, 2007). It proposes large infrastructural programmes, which include roads, railways, airports, seaports, special economic zones and building of the Konza techno-city. The Vision has, however, not freed itself from the top-down catch-up modernisation trend. It has ignored the African logic and institutions input and is pegged on foreign investors, imported technology, western and oriental philosophies. It's not inclusive as it only meets the needs of the middle class rather than that of the massive lower class and those operating in the informal sector.

There has also been widespread development activism to transform peasant activities in rural areas. NGOs such as SACDEP and Farm Input Promotions Africa have initiated programmes to support peasant agriculture. These include research on improved seeds, dissemination of market information and farmer training. Other programmes include the Shamba Shape-up programme, a telecast TV programme that targets peasant farmers. It involves actual site visits to farmers who are taught by a crew of experts on how to modernise their farming. Some initiatives impart agribusiness skills to wean peasant farmers off subsistence farming and encourage value addition to farm produce. Essentially, these programmes introduce farmers to capitalist production, seed and pesticide supply chains. The *Daily Nation* newspaper's pull-out feature called *Seeds of Gold* highlights successful farmers with the hope that others can learn from their best practices.

For a majority of artisans and traders, peasants, the fisherfolk, little has changed in the logic and institutions of doing business in economic informality, except for the adoption of mobile telephony and money transfer (Mensah and Wangai 2011). It is our contention that this failure is attributable to the fact that most policies do not address Wanjiku's needs. Instead, they marginalise and peripherise or ignore the complexity of the African logic and institutions in the design and formulation of the policies. For example, The World Bank voucher training programme ignored the complexities in the *jua kali* training programmes and fronted consultants who were not business people. Jointly financed by the World Bank and the Kenya Government, the Kenya Micro and Small Enterprise Training and Technology Project (MSETTP) was launched in November 1994. The Kenya Jua Kali Voucher Program was the largest component of the MSETTP. The voucher program focused attention on the skill upgrading needs of the Jua Kali sector with a view of improving the productivity of micro and small enterprises as well as the incomes of entrepreneurs and their employees. While the Ministry of Research, Technical Training and Technology (MRTT&T) was responsible for the project, the Project Coordination Office (PCO) comprising private consultants and MRTT&T staff was created to implement the project.

Economic informality however continues to entrench itself in urban economies (Kinyanjui, 2014). The ordinary citizenry continue to encroach into the city (Ngwala, 2011, Kinyanjui, 2013, 2014). Malls are embracing Maasai markets into their premises. In rural areas, the majority of the people still derive their livelihoods from land as peasants.

Development studies such as the work of Todaro (1994) observe that there is a widespread production for subsistence and little accumulation of wealth. Production and exchange are geared towards survival and subsistence. Most of the production and exchange is not monetised or geared towards the self-regulating market. The postcolonial perspective proposes that peasants, artisans and traders' production is outside non-capitalist due to the fact that they produce for subsistence and survival; and hence they are poor and need to be incorporated into the global capitalist circuits or socialist models of production. Where there is a link between peasants, artisans and traders' production and exchange with capitalist firms and farms, there is pervasive systemic exploitation.

There is a possibility of a non-capitalist agency to preserve Wanjiku's mode of production and exchange. Wanjiku has many times resisted total incorporation to capitalist production and exchange. She has resisted wholesale transformation and preferred to adapt her institutions to the self-regulating market and money culture. Examples of such adaptation include the Susu in West Africa and *chama* (welfare group) in Kenya. She has also tried to maintain the institution of the African market in the city. While she recognises the importance of transformation, she maintains her values and identity. In the liberation struggle in the 1950s, while the elite wanted to be treated with dignity and sit at table with the white people, Wanjiku wanted *wiyathi* (self-governance) and *ithaka* (land). She wanted self-rule, not the exploitative rule of the *njuhiga* (the cunning ones). She wanted to create her own institutions, and build her own production exchange and surplus disposal. That is why she easily mobilised into land buying companies, building schools and hospitals through harambees and in the process creating social formation that would help realise *wiyathi na ithaka* (self-governance and land).

The elite in the post-colony performed just like the colonialist towards Wanjiku by perpetuating a social formation that relied on state apparatus to extract surplus from her. The elite endeavoured to capture Wanjiku through strategies similar to those of colonial exploitation, such as setting up marketing boards to cream off surplus. The first form of dissatisfaction with elite governance was a song by Gathaithi Church Choir:

Ona riu Mai nimaruru. (The water is bitter.)

Ni marurutukunyuaki? (It is bitter. What shall we drink?)

Wathiewabicikuhoyauteithio, (If you go to an office to seek help,)

Ugakoramundumurakaru. (You find an angry person.)

*Woigauingiriagakwirandi*busy. (When you request to get in, he says he is busy.)

Another one: *Nyota maita nyota no nyota* (Thirst times, thirst is thirst) was against the excessive desire of leaders to accumulate wealth. The song warned that this was like a bottomless pit, or like thirst, which even after being quenched, will come back. Through these songs, peasants expressed their disgust with the bourgeoise-led government, which does not deliver services but who leaders were keen on accumulating personal wealth.

The new constitutions that were crafted to restructure the post-colony governance structures were neither ideologically nor philosophically different from those of the post-colonial state. The 2010 Kenyan Constitution did not wean itself from the philosophy or the ideology of the elite-led governance and development paradigms of the post-colonial state. It is still an elite-formulated constitution that does not question the mode of production and accumulation prevailing in the country. It may be good for service and infrastructure delivery, but it does not deal with the mode of production, exchange and accumulation that Wanjiku uses. While acknowledging and reviving the institutions of elders, it excludes elders and other people who have been supporting local schools by insisting that school boards must be composed of individuals with secondary education or higher. It also embraces neo-liberalism and liberal democracy as defined in western cultures. It does not eliminate the postcolonial dilemma of liberal bourgeois failing to lead the revolution, power formation and transformation. It does not include Wanjiku's social and economic ethos of production, exchange and accumulation.

It is important to reconcile Wanjiku's exchange and production, well-being and wealth with that of corporations' and governments in the new global economy. It would also be important to enhance the global economic thought with Wanjiku's economic logic, norms and values that have ensured their continued survival in Africa while the rest of the global economy has been subject to multiple crises which have seen them depend on the government for bailouts.

Unfortunately, in the new millennium, the condition of a large majority of peasants in Kenya is pathetic, especially among the coffee farmers (Kamau 2015; Kinyanjui 2015; Mbataru 2016). These commentators have documented peasant struggles and exploitation in coffee production in Kenya. Their stories describe how the peasant coffee farmers have been exploited at the coffee markets, which are dominated by brokers and cartels, both local and international.

The top-down development, catch-up capitalistic models proposed in the modernisation and liberalisation paradigms for positioning women peasants, traders and artisans in the global economy are exploitative. There is need to search for alternative methods that they can use to position themselves in the money culture and self-regulating markets in the global economy. Their logic and norms in production and exchange in farming, craft and trade, as well as their agency, resilience and insurgency in the determination of well-being, wealth and circulation of money in the household and in the community.

This necessitates the need to address the question of Wanjiku's wealth and well-being in the new millennium. Key questions such as the following come to mind: why does Wanjiku continue to engage in production and exchange in a globalised economy that marginalises and exploits her? What are her values? What is her version of capitalism? How does she achieve self-actualisation? What is her perspective on wealth and wellbeing? What are her trade-offs in money circulation? What is the basis of the sustainability of her production and exchange? How does she relate to the national and global economy?

The positioning of Wanjiku in the restructuring of the global economy can be illuminated by the works of Polanyi (1944), who is a critic of the capitalistic transformation that took place in Europe in the 19th Century. He observes the Great Transformation where craft production was transformed into corporations through the power of a self-regulating market and the entrenchment of the culture of money. He documents the spread and entrenchment of the self-regulating market, money culture and the double movements which made land and labour artificial commodities that could be traded in the market. The question is: has the modernisation and liberalisation of Wanjiku's production and exchange taken the route defined by Polanyi?

Perhaps the missing input in the post-colonial engagement with Wanjiku is the failure to consider the issue of her trauma, restoration and transformation. The violence, disruption and dislocation Wanjiku encountered were immense. Demands for wholesale acculturation meant peasant insurgency in such places as in Dagoretti District led by Waiyaki Wahinga (Kinyatti, 2019) Oral narratives of this violence persist. Others include the Lari Massacre in 1953 Ndungu (2011), the burning of Githunguri Teachers College and the banning of Independent Schools by the government (Wairia, 2006). Even today, there are villages in Central Province known as *kwa aregi* - the place of insurgents.

At the intersection of the new global economy, we are again making the same choices: whether to embrace western mass consumerism and global corporation investment, or continue with Wanjiku's production and exchange or a hybrid of the two modes of production. Should the latter be positioned as an alternative to global capitalism and mass consumerism?

CHAPTER FIVE

WANJIKU IN THE EVERYDAY LIVELIHOOD NEGOTIATIONS

Wanjiku is involved in everyday livelihood survival activities in trade, artisanry, (animal and crop) husbandry and real estate. Activities like trade, artisanry and farming are indigenous livelihood activities which she has articulated to global development. Others like real estate are new and she is trying to adapt to or integrate as part of her participation in global development. She brings in her logic and solidarities as methods and institutions of survival. For our study, the ordinary livelihood activities which Wanjiku engages in are drawn from Kimalel goat auction, sorghum trade in Kakamega, Kisii soapstone artisan work, Gatukuyu Coffee Cooperative, Kienyeji chicken farming, Dagoretti Plot Owners Association, Usare beach fish trading and Kamukunji Jua Kali organisation. Wanjiku engages in heterogeneous activities and sometimes uses similar logic and solidarities in everyday livelihood survival. The case studies used in this book do not represent overall views of women in livelihood survival. They express complexity and lessons that can be learnt from the individual women who were purposively selected on the basis of their willingness to hold conversations with the researcher.

Kimalel Goat Auction

The Kimalel Goat Auction takes place every December in Baringo County. The county is mainly arid and is situated in Kenya's Rift Valley region. In the 2019 Census, the County had 666,763 people of which 336,322 were male and 330,428 were female (Kenya Population and Housing Census, 2019).

It is inhabited by the Tugen (who form the dominant ethnic community), Pokot, Ilchamus, Turkana, Nubians and Kikuyu. Kabarnet is its main town.

Dominant economic activities in the country include tourism, agriculture and livestock keeping. Food crops such as Irish potatoes, sweet potatoes, maize, pigeon peas, cassava, sorghum and finger millet are grown. Pastoralism is still dominant in the region and involves the rearing of indigenous goats and cows which graze in open range lands. Traditionally, goats would be exchanged for foodstuffs and were an indicator of wealth. They were also used for payment of bride wealth.

The fact that Daniel Arap Moi, the second president of Kenya, who ruled for 24 years, came from Baringo, makes the understanding of the area's marginalisation in global development fairly complex. Baringo's incorporation into global capitalist development is further complicated by its climatic conditions and the resilience of the Tugen and the Ilchamus to preserve their autonomy and indigeneity. Frequent conflicts flare up in Baringo as different groups fight for the survival of autonomy and indigeneity. One of the economic goals of colonialism was to extract labour, resources and destroy indigeneity by introducing new cultures and technologies through the power of the gun. Communities that had strong armies and harsh environments withstood invasive colonial occupation and extraction of labour and resources. Unable to fully occupy Baringo, the colonial government reserved and gazetted it as a forest. For these reasons, some of their indigenous practices such as pastoralism have survived into the 21 Century.

In the postcolonial state, pastoral communities became even more marginalised. On a field trip with Geography students from Kenyatta University in 1988, we visited many sites and development projects in Baringo to be apprised on efforts to arrest the marginalisation of Baringo and environmental degradation by the Kerio Valley Development Authority (KVDA). Most of the projects in the development authority aimed at controlling soil erosion, agroforestry, sedentary lifestyles and encouraging crop farming for the majority of pastoral communities. There were also programmes for destocking so that the animal land carrying capacity could be improved. Attempts were also made to promote tourism by making Lake Baringo a tourist site. The Kenya Tourism Development Corporation (KTDC) was charged with the responsibility of constructing hotels. Other activities that were to be promoted were mining and geothermal energy extraction. There were widespread efforts to promote education and infrastructure.

In another visit to Baringo in 2016, one of the things that I observed was the emergence of women market traders by the roadsides selling mangoes, honey and bananas. Some agroforestry had taken place and gullies were not as glaring as they had been in 1988. Guest houses and new hotels had been constructed and rectangular iron-sheet and brick houses were replacing traditional mud houses. There were also new schools, both public and private. Many cows and goats were still grazing in the open spaces. The above scenarios demonstrate increasing evidence of movement towards incorporation into the global capitalist production.

Some more focus on the Kimalel Goat Auction in Baringo follows below. The relevant government departments that have a direct or peripheral association with the auction include planning and agriculture,among others.

Under the devolved government, Baringo County is committed to continue with the neoliberal global development in its vision and mission. Baringo County's vision is to be the most attractive competitive and resilient County that affords the highest standard of living and security for all residents. The county's mission is to transform the livelihoods of Baringo residents by creating a conducive framework that offers quality services in a fair equitable and transparent manner embracing community managed development initiatives for environmental stability, adaptable technologies, innovation end entrepreneurship in all spheres of life.

The objectives of the economic planning department and those of the agriculture, livestock development further spell out these neoliberal approaches to global development in Baringo ((Baringo County, 2013). The mission of the economic planning department is to be excellent in county economic planning and public finance while its mission is to contribute towards accelerated economic development through effective economic planning, resource mobilisation and allocations of resources, management of public resources. The specific objectives of the department include finance management efficiency, strengthening of institutions and good governance, resource mobilisation, public private partnerships and allocation of resources, creation of excellent delivery of service.

The agriculture, livestock and fisheries department's vision and mission equally enhanced a neoliberal approach to global development. The vision envisions a food secure, competitive and productive County while the mission envisages improved livelihoods through promotion of competitive agriculture, innovative research and growth of the viable cooperative sector. The department has several objectives some of which include to promote adoption of appropriate technologies for crops, livestock and fisheries, increase productivity through facilitating access to affordable and quality input services; and increase market access through promotion of value addition and development of standards along value chain.

A neoliberal approach to global development is also applied by the county's gender, youth sport and disability department. Its vision is to make Baringo a leading county in creating an economically empowered gender responsive and socially protected community while its mission is to reduce dependency through the socio-economic empowerment of youth, women and vulnerable groups. One of its objectives is to empower women financially through inculcation of entrepreneurial skills, provision of loans, social protection to the elderly, orphans and persons with disability.

Introducing neoliberal approaches to global development in communities that have struggled to preserve their indigeneity for so long is not easy. One of the failures of these approach is reflected in the fact that out of the Kshs 11,265,502 available for disbursement to youth and women in the county, very little had been disbursed, a clear sign of resistance to the approaches in 2013. It is also important to note that livestock, although a dominant feature in most households in Baringo, ranks seventh (Kshs 15,254,617) in revenue contribution to the county. The most important source of revenue contribution in the county were hospital services (Kshs 84,000,000) followed by game park services (Kshs 74,356,033). In terms of economic activities contribution to revenue in Baringo, livestock ranks fifth after market fees (Kshs 50,647,583), single business permit (Kshs 48,577,208), plot rates and rents (Kshs 39,203,758), produce cess (Kshs 38,561,801), animal stock sales (Kshs 15,253,617).

This somewhat might be indicative of the lack of willingness of the households to let go of their livelihood – livestock. Moreover, Kimalel Goat Auction, a major economic feature that attracts a lot of attention in Baringo and nationally due to the volumes of money involved as shown later in the chapter, is not mentioned in the financial report development objectives.

The Kimalel Goat Auction is a yearly event carried out in Baringo County. It was initiated by the community elite to introduce goats, an indigenous commodity, into the market. In 1986, President Daniel Arap Moi introduced the goat auction to help create fair conditions in goat trade. Today it is a great event that brings together Kalenjin elites drawn from politics, business and different professions. They all troop Baringo to purchase goats from ordinary Kalenjin livestock farmers.

The evolution of the auction was in part in response to what was happening with livestock from the region. Urbanisation had opened up new markets for meat in different parts of the country. However, since most pastoralists could not make it to markets in urban centres, a cadre of brokers who interfaced between them and markets evolved. The brokers would buy the goats cheaply and then sell them expensively to butchers in towns. As a result, many of the goat keepers were not making profits from their goats.

When the goat auction started in 1986, it was largely a men's affair as in this community, goats were owned by men. They were a measure of the man's wealth. Unlike, farming communities who were quickly recruited into farming for crops for exports, pastoral communities were largely left out in the modernisation and neoliberal programmes.

The goat auction is a deliberate move to articulate an indigenous commodity into global development, monetise goat keeping, and ensure that pastoralists trade their goats in a fair and open market devoid of exploitation by brokers. The latter came mainly from Nairobi. The pastoralists aggregate their goats at Kimalel Goat Auction, aggregates of which are sold to buyers.

President Moi used to attend the yearly goat auction, which also turned out to be an important political event where the elite show off their power and wealth and extend some benevolence to the ordinary livestock farmers. In 2015 and 2016, Kenya's Deputy President, William Samoei Ruto, attended the auction. This well-attended event is also a space of interaction between the elite and the ordinary pastoralists. The elite who earn their income in towns bring it home in exchange for goats. It is a form of giving back and redistribution to community.

The preparation of goats for participation in the auction is an all-year event that involves veterinary officers, agricultural extension officers, and sponsors. The goats have to be of a certain weight in order to participate in the auction, which is sponsored by Kenya Commercial Bank. This is also a way of encouraging financial inclusion and integration of the pastoralist community. Most of them deposit their earnings from the auction in Kenya Commercial Bank.

According to a 2015 report in *The Standard* newspaper, Deputy President William Ruto observed that the auction provides an easy market for farmers by eliminating middlemen. It also accords farmers an opportunity to showcase their livestock, network, market their produce, and learn best practises in livestock farming. "Promoting food security and reducing extreme poverty in Arid and Semi-Arid (Asal) regions is a key priority for the government. As a government, we intend to help pastoral communities increase their adaptive capacity and resilience to produce high-quality agricultural and livestock produce," said Mr Ruto during the auction. In 2014, the goat auction raised 18.7 million Kenya shillings. In 2015, (24 million) and 30 million Kenya shillings in 2016 (Koech and Kipsang, 2017).

The auction initially involved men but women are slowly making inroads into it. The majority of the women who enter the goat market are widowed or single due to divorce. The women enter the goat market from a disadvantaged position and usually have a smaller number of goats compared to men.

Dorcas Rerimoi said she had to pay extra cash to transport back her 22 goats to Sibilo, fifty kilometres away from the market centre. She hoped to raise some cash to pay her children's school fees. Gideon Cherop, one of the traders, brought 200 goats for sale but got disappointed to find the gates locked. "I am a livestock farmer as well as a businessman. I don't know where to find another ready market to sell my goats after missing out the annual goat auction," Cherop said. (Kangongo and Vidija, 2016).

The woman had 22 goats while the man had 200. The woman brought the goats to the auction to raise money for school fees. Her articulation into the goat auction was closely tied to her reproduction and nurturing roles. The man, who identified himself as a businessman, was participating in the goat auction to build his business empire. Three women participating in the Kimalel goat action will demonstrate how they articulate their solidarity and logic of nurturing in this new development in the county.

Sorghum Farmers in Kakamega

In 2019, Kakamega County had a population of 1,867,579 people. There were 897,133 male and 970,406 females (Kenya Population and Housing Census, 2019). Kakamega County has nine major markets. Sorghum is an indigenous grain crop that is grown in many parts of Africa. Unlike in Central Kenya where indigenous crops were shunned on modernisation grounds, most parts of Western, Eastern, North Eastern and Rift Valley areas of Kenya have maintained some of their indigenous crop and livestock farming. Scientific research and livestock development usually starts with a premise that Flora and Fauna in the continent is unproductive, unhealthy and difficult to commercialise in modern markets. Until recently, eating indigenous foods was considered backward. However, some communities are still practising indigenous crop and livestock farming. Some have commercialised these. Some of the indigenous crops maintained in these regions include *mrenda, manage,* sorghum, millet, cassava and varieties of sugarcane. The Zebu cow and traditional goats have also been maintained.

Most of the indigenous crops and livestock are sold by market traders rather than marketing boards. Andole and Maatsui (2019) observe that market trade attracts a majority of women in Kakamega. Kakamega Municipal Market is the largest in the County and is located in Kakamega Town. The main market days are Wednesdays and Saturdays. Most of the women commute to the market from their rural farms.

Andole and Maatsui (2019) observe that the women traders were aged between 21 and 50 years and majority had primary and secondary school education. They also earned between Kshs 20,000 ($200) and 30,000 ($300) per month from the market trade. Unfortunately, the volume of market trade is largely undocumented because modern economics do not consider the activity significant or important enough for food security or global capitalist development.

The county's vision is to be wealthy, vibrant and offer high quality services to its residents. Its mission is to improve the welfare of the people of Kakamega County through formulation and implementation of all-inclusive multi-sectoral policies (Kakamega County, 2018). The County does not recognise market trade as part of its global capitalist development. Apart from the construction of modern markets, there is very little else to promote market trade. In the report, promotion of tourism, agriculture, environmental conservation are embraced but not market trade where a large majority of women are involved.

Sorghum is used for food and making beer. Until recently, it was considered a low income household food. The modern household food basket consisted of maize products or rice. Sorghum is low in sugar and is therefore good for diabetics and individuals interested in weight loss. Sorghum is ground into flour to make *ugali,* porridge or beer. Traditionally it was ground using stone or mortar and pestle. Today, it is ground in posho mills, that are usually family owned. Some modern firms are taking up sorghum grinding and packaging it for sale in supermarkets. Otherwise, most of sorghum flour is sold in African markets.

Cereals and grains were traditionally associated with women. They were grown to meet their gender specific roles of nurturing and feeding the family. They were also bartered to buy household goods such as pots or fish. With colonialism, women adopted cash instead of barter trade in African markets. Today, women play an important role in marketing sorghum grains and flour in African markets in most urban centres. The women have articulated sorghum into global capitalist development through their own initiatives and self-determination. Three women are drawn from the Kakamega Municipal market to illustrate how they articulate their logic of solidarity and nurturing in trade.

Kisii Soapstone, Tabaka. Kisii County

One of the pre-colonial craftwork that has survived to this day is the mining of soapstone and making of curios from soapstone at Tabaka in Kisii County (Akama and Onyambu, 2018). The Kisii community is situated in the South Western part of Kenya. Soapstone craft work has evolved into a commercial activity upon which many families derive their income. Most of the craft products include animals, key holders, flower vases, trays, candle holders, game boards and pen holders, among others. These are sold in local tourist hotels or exported abroad. Kisii soapstone artisans' production is a traditional art and craft that garners millions of shillings.

The craft work has an integrated process that has a marked division of labour. The process involves mining, rock selection, carving, sanding, decoration and polishing. Most of the mining and carving is carried out by men, while women engage in washing, drying, waxing, polishing, sanding and selection of rocks. Some women are also breaking into male craft processes of carving and painting. The craft work is also organised around families and sometimes passed from one generation to the next. Most of the income generated from the business is used for domestic consumption: providing food, shelter, education and meeting health expenses. An estimated

15,000 families residing in the Tabaka hills depend on the craft for income. (Onyambu and Akama 2018)

Onyambu and Akama (2018) notes that there have been many false starts over the years to solidify the Tabaka soapstone trade. The false starts have seen the soapstone craft societies crumble as a result of leaders' self-interest and the evolution of soapstone craft from a utilitarian value to aesthetic, largely due to mass produced industrial products imported from the West. Efforts are however being made to integrate Tabaka craft production into global financial circuits through cooperatives. The Tabaka cooperative encourages the community to address community challenges such as lack of money, dropping out of school, early pregnancies, child labour, unemployment and HIV/Aids. The cooperative lobbies for better wages for artisans, safe and decent working conditions, health insurance and skills training. It also encourages the saving of 15% of members' income. Efforts are also being made to link up with importers from Fair Trade organisations as a strategy for positioning the artisans in the global economy.

Kamukunji Jua Kali Cluster in Nairobi

Kamukunji Jua Kali (fierce sun) artisan cluster is a metal product processing hub for the production of household and agricultural goods. According to Mr. Fredrick Dawa, former secretary general of the Kamukunji Jua Kali Association, there are about 4,000 people operating in the cluster. They include artisans, trainees, brokers and casual workers. About 85% of the people are men and 15% are women. They make many products such as metal boxes, wheelbarrows, potato chip cutters, chips warmers, popcorn poppers, chicken feeders, chaff cutters, pans, cooking stoves, and cooking pots among others. Most of the products are sold to low income populations in Nairobi and rural areas. Some of the products like wheelbarrows are exported to Congo, Uganda, Rwanda and Tanzania.

Kamukunji's tenacity at the heart of the city is a surprise to many. Its evolution in the city is attributable to blacksmith activities which were recognised as part of hawking in the 1928 Hawkers Bylaw. Artisan works were integrated into the colonial urban economy to cater for the needs of the African population (Kinyanjui, 2009). In the early days, the artisans repaired household goods, made stoves, tin lamps and pans. In the 1960s, former Mau Mau detainees who had acquired skills in detention joined the cluster. By 1970, there were 150 artisans operating in the cluster. In 1985 the number had increased to 350 (Kamukunji Jua Kali Website). In the 1990s, the artisans had been joined by individuals who lost jobs in the metal sector after the collapse of the import substitution industries in the country. The growth of the cluster is also enhanced by recent rural urban migrants who are brought into the cluster by relatives and friends. They all undergo a thorough socialisation process.

Anecdotal information has it that President Daniel Arap Moi had gone to watch a football match at the neighbouring Nyayo Stadium one Sunday afternoon in 1986. He was attracted by the deafening noise of hammers that were pounding metal sheets at Kamukunji. He went to see what was happening in the small area and found many people, young and old, manufacturing household goods and agricultural implements. Sympathising with their poor working conditions, his first impulse was to construct sheds for them and later apportion them land. He asked them to form an association. He also created the Ministry of Applied Technology and Training to handle their affairs in 1988. The Kenya Federation of Jua Kali Artisans was also formed to be an umbrella organisation for all *jua kali* associations in the country. The federation also incorporated other East African countries and holds annual exhibitions on a rotational basis among member countries.

This effort renewed interest in the informal sector in the country, which had somewhat gone into a lull after its initial highlighting by Hart (1973) and ILO (1972). The World Bank initiated the Voucher Training Programme while the UNDP embarked on programmes for entrepreneurship training, opening up demonstration centres and providing equipment and machines to *jua kali* artisans and mechanics. One of the beneficiaries of the UNDP machine and equipment programmes was Ziwani vehicle garage locally known as Kaburi and the Kariobangi demonstration centre in the 1994.

Situated in the freedom ceremonial grounds of Kamukunji, the *jua kali* fraternity is amazing. How do they make cooking stoves, pots, pans, wheelbarrows, metal boxes, chips cutters, hoes, *pangas*, popcorn poppers, gutters, cooking pots, and stoves, among other products? How do they weather so many economic, policy and social shocks? How do they balance ethnic and gender interests? How do they balance age differences and political affiliations? How do they minimise conflicts? How do they adjust to innovations and competition from other sectors? How do they carry out training programmes for future artisans?

Women have made inroads into the cluster as owners of businesses, employees in polishing and painting as well as sales persons. Some are also learning craft work. The ability of the cluster to survive lies in its complex internal organisation, rural-urban linkage, and inspirational subaltern African consciousness. Some have been hardened by the trauma of neglect by modernisation, and neoliberal policies. They take their hardening positively, engage in gainful action, negotiate change in chats or formal meetings, and change at their own terms. The issue at hand is whether they will survive the cheap imports from China and the government's initiative of establishing business, vocational and technical training.

The three women artisans from Kamukunji in this book narrate their articulation into global development. Women join the cluster through family links or through their own initiatives. The latter illustrates their genius in the identification of a growing sector that will hasten their entry into the money culture that aligns with their logic, norms and values of going into business.

Kienyeji Chicken Farmers in Machakos

Kienyeji (indigenous) chicken farmers from Ukambani have articulated traditional free range chicken in global development through urban-rural trader networks. Kienyeji chicken rearing is common in most rural households in Kenya. Magothe et al., (2012) observe that indigenous chicken production in very common in Kenya and Machakos is on the counties with a lot of chicken. In traditional society, chicken were used for spiritual cleansing, healing rituals and also for sports such as cock fighting (Magothe et al, 2012). While most of the chicken is kept for household consumption, with increased urbanisation and demand for increased health foods, rural households sell their chicken into this market. Every day, thousands of chicken are transferred from Ukambani to Nairobi. Most of this trade goes on undocumented. In residential estates, one will find a chicken coop where live Kienyeji chicken are sold. Unlike parts of Central Kenya that adopted modern chicken layers and broilers, many households in Machakos retained their own indigenous chicken. These are women's livestock. In the morning, the women open the hen pen and leave them to feed on the range. In the evening, the chicken come back home to roost and the woman's role is to shut them in and collect the eggs. Initially, they are kept for eggs, and meat for household consumption.

Many urban residents also carry chicken to the city while returning from rural areas. Someone might have identified the demand and decided to stock the chicken in the city. Indigenous chicken are preferred because of their low-fat content, better taste, ability to be reared without use of antibiotics, and fibrous flesh. Scientists have tried to improve the indigenous breed but its adoption is slow because most consumers prefer the traditional breed.

Trade in chicken might have begun in Nairobi as early as 1928 when African traders and artisans were allowed to trade in the city. Trade in indigenous chicken has increased over time and it is not unusual to see public transport vehicles from Machakos carrying chicken on their roof racks. Through these methods, Kienyeji chicken production has been articulated into global development. Three women are used in this book to illustrate how they have articulated their logic and solidarities in this global development project.

Usare Beach Lake Victoria, Kisumu County

Lake Victoria is a large fresh water lake, the largest such lake in Africa, situated in East Africa. It straddles across Kenya, Uganda and Tanzania. Usare beach, one of the fish-landing bays in Kisumu on the Kenyan side has a large representation of artisanal fishing. Fishing is an important economic activity in Kisumu County. Fishing creates jobs for both men and women. It is carried out mainly by men. Women mainly trade in fish. The women collect the fish from the bays early in the morning and take it to the markets in the neighbouring counties. Before the colonial period, fishing was mainly for household consumption and market trade with other communities.

While fishing is still a male occupation, women are making inroads into the activity as boat owners, fish cleaners and fish dryers. Large scale commercial fishing was initiated with the introduction of the Nile perch into the lake in the 1950s by the colonial government. Most of the Nile perch is exported to Europe and also sold in large markets in urban centres susch as Nairobi and Mombasa. Fish indigenous to the lake include Tilapia, *Omena* and Mud Fish. A lot of women trade in these indigenous fish types (Kamau et al 2012). Artisanal fishing, which is manually done or done using power boats, is still dominant in the lake. Motorised boats are gradually taking over the manually operated boats. Investors are buying motor boats and commissioning fishermen to go out into the lake. Some of these investors include women who are realising the importance of having their own money.

Fishing, an indigenous activity, has also been articulated into global development. To control and extract labour, Nile perch was introduced into the lake to meet the demand of export markets during the colonial period. The government has also tried further to integrate fishing into global development by having fishing as a major department in the ministry of livestock.

Beach management associations with elected officials manage and run the beaches (Mitullah 1999). The beach management keeps the record of the fishermen, sets rules and regulations for regulating the operations within the beaches, deals with conflicts, and links fishermen with the government fisheries departments (Kamau, 2012; Mitullah, 1999). It also ensures that the environment at the beach is not polluted. Unfortunately, women representation in the beach management leadership is poor.

Mitullah's study (Mitullah, 1999) on the role of collective efficiency and joint action in Lake Victoria fishing beaches observed that effective institutions had failed to evolve in the fishing beaches and that the beach association could not address the power relations that characterised the emerging crises. The beach cooperative and fisheries departments were weak institutions due to the government's efforts to capture and articulate an indigenous activity into global development. Three women from Usare beach are used to demonstrate how they articulate their logic of self-determination and nurturing in fish trade.

Dagoretti District Plot Owners

Dagoretti Plot Owners Association draws membership from a community living on their ancestral land in the Nairobi neighbourhood. They have shifted from relying on farming to real estate housing production. Dagoretti District is not made of migrant communities like the rest of the city. It was incorporated in the Nairobi city boundary through a presidential directive in 1969. It was hived off from the now Kiambu County. Unfortunately, no major urban development projects were put in place to transform the basically rural place. Individual plot owners have been engaging in urban development by building houses for rent. The majority of these houses are for low income urban residents.

Dagoretti plot owners are descendants of an indigenous community that was found in this locality by Captain Lugard when he established Fort Smith. There has been a long history of resistance and collaboration as the community seeks to adjust to modernity, urbanisation and global capitalist production.

In my journal entry on my visit to Muthua chief's camp on 14th February, 2015 described earlier, the mixture of modernity and traditional African practices coexisting is a portrayal of insurgency and resilience. The community attempts to configure its own incorporation into modernity and capitalist development. The resistance started with the open conflict between Chief Waiyaki wa Hinga and the British colonialists. Waiyaki was later arrested and buried alive at Kibwezi. Resistance changed with the installation of chief Kinyanjui wa Gathirimu who collaborated with the British (Kinyatti, 2019). There is also a considerable growing elite and middle class in the area. However, most of the residents are peasants, artisans or traders. This is safe for their entry into the real estate as low income suppliers of houses. There is also a growing crop of depeasantised male who are educated but cannot get jobs. Most of the indigenous Dagoretti people do not want to lose their ancestral properties and inheritance. They want to be in control of who resides in their compounds rather than giving their houses to agents. They do not want to mortgage their land or use it as collateral. Public education is poor, so a majority cannot go that route of modernisation and entry into the money culture. They choose to construct *mabati* housing which they rent out for money. The houses are passed on to their sons and daughters as inheritance. We shall see how three women break cultural barriers to inherit land and own rental houses in Dagoretti.

Githunguri Dairy Cooperative

Githunguri is a rural town in Kiambu County that specialises in milk processing. The town houses four milk processing factories namely Palmhouse Dairies, Githunguri Dairy Farmers Cooperative, Kinyagi and Upland Milk Processors. Palmhouse Dairies, Kinyagi and Upland Milk Processors are family-owned businesses while Githunguri Dairy Farmers Cooperative is owned by small scale milk producers from the area. Palmhouse Dairies was the first company to engage in milk production in the area followed by Githunguri Dairy Farmers Cooperative. Most of the milk produced in Githunguri is consumed in Nairobi. The four factories in Githunguri have generated significant multiplier effects that indirectly affect rural women in areas such as food supply, cattle rearing, animal feeds supply and retail trade.

Milk processing is sustained by the constant supply of milk from the small-scale farmers in the area. The success of milk processing in Githunguri is due to the existence of a large market in Nairobi, the adoption of new technologies, sound management practices and the commitment, solidarity and loyalty of the small-scale farmers to the cooperative.

Githunguri Dairy Cooperative was established in 1961 by 31 members, all of them men. The members were inspired by the liberation struggle that aimed at enabling Africans to own the means of production rather than be servile workers in European settler firms and farms. The aspiration to be independent, control production, and be self-reliant was highly fronted by the Gikuyu Karing'a education movement in the area which embraced both Western education and African values. Western education introduced them to reading, writing and arithmetic while African values introduced them to self-reliance, self-determination hard work, fairness and solidarity. The movement also drew inspiration from the black economic movement in the United States. The first Principal of Githunguri Teachers College, Mbiyu Koinange, had attended Hampton College where he learnt technical and vocational skills. At its inception, the cooperative was led by visionary people who had a strong mix of Christianity and African traditional values. The leaders used their knowledge, natural resources and social networks to better the cooperative. They accommodated both the smallholder farmer with the least output in milk production as well as the farmer with more milk. Working for the common good of the members of the cooperative was given pre-eminence. This effort was a form of anti-colonial resistance that was transformational and preserved the peasant values of solidarity, family and community flourishing. The cooperative emphasised independence over state control. Its leaders were not allowed to hold government elective positions. This was to guard against political and divisive influence. The community in which the cooperative operated was supportive and owned the development process. Some of the peasants donated their parcels of land to be used as milk collection centres. They provided pick-up vans to collect milk from farmers to deliver to the Kenya Cooperative Creameries.

According to one respondent from Githunguri, what she does was passed on to her by her parents. She said she would in turn pass it to her children. Another respondent observed that female children receive animal husbandry skills from their mothers. She observed that her daughter, a university student, milks their cows. She advises people to learn multiple skills and do all types of work such as cutting napier grass, feeding animals, cleaning the cowshed and milking. The two respondents point towards a process of socialisation that transfers skills, attitude, logic and norms to the next generation.

The cooperative's mode of production combines modernity, capitalism and African logic and norms. It has 24,000 registered members. The active ones as of 19-11-2016 were 13,768. During its October 22,2016 Annual General Meeting, 12,293 members attended. Of these attendees, the number of Male members were 6,319 while females were 5,974. Dormant number 10,486,6,136 male and 4,350, female. Most of the dormant ones include those whose cows no longer produce milk and those who supply milk to other factories in Githunguri.

Key factors that have sustained the cooperative include mandatory monthly forums and a milk collection system based on ridges. The area is divided into routes based on the geographical feature - the ridge and the traditional political organisation of Gikuyu communities. Route one: Githunguri; Route two: Kambaa; Route three: Githiga; Route four: Ikunu; Route five: Gathanji; Route six: Ngewa; Route seven: Gitiha; Route eight: Gakoe; Route nine: Gathaithi. People occupying one ridge are likely to be connected though blood, marriage or religion. This makes integration easier. The milk routes ease milk collection and management of members. Each zone is managed by a director who supervises the activities of the zone, holds monthly meetings and represents the zone in the cooperative management board. Ridges in the precolonial society were divided according to different clans and cultural practices. People from one ridge would undergo initiation rites together and hence bond, monitor each other and castigate wrong doing. In each ridge, there are several sub routes. Milk collection points are situated within a walking distance of homes, usually not more than two kilometres. There are about 80 milk collecting centres. Each route has a code.

Learning is an important ingredient of the cooperative management. It involves training on handling feeds, maintaining cleanliness in milking and adoption of new technologies like making biogas from human and animal waste. The cooperative has recruited about 14 dairy extension officers who treat animals, carry out artificial insemination, control the quality of milk and enforce hygiene standards. They are also taught on efficient management of fodder, record keeping, formulation of feeds, bull selection, control of diseases such as mastitis and udder disease, management of zero grazing unit and calf management.

The cooperative has 58 feed stores. Members can access feeds through credit check-off systems. The cooperative offers good prices, pays regularly without delays, and gives farmers bonuses at the end of each year. If a farmer has delivered 10,000 litres in a year, he or she can earn as much as Kshs 20,000 as bonus. Annual dividends are also given on performance.

The cooperative started by supplying milk to the now defunct Kenya Cooperative Creameries (KCC). When the Kenya Cooperative Creameries collapsed, Githunguri Dairy Cooperative moved to milk hawking in the city and later started value addition of their milk under the Fresha brand.

The cooperative is managed by a board of directors who are elected by the members. It has an executive committee comprising of the chairman, secretary and treasurer. Each board member represents a milk route. Every month, the route director holds meetings with cooperative members of the area. Every year, the cooperative holds an Annual General Meeting where policies are reviewed and reading of accounts and future innovations discussed. The cooperative has a system of laws and regulations that are formulated by the members. The members also determine the sanctions to be administered to law breakers. Implementation of any changes is approved by consensus. The members discuss the budget, introduction of new feeds, employment of workers, animal medicines, expansion, creation of other institutions such as a SACCO to support buying of property, education, insurance, and welfare. To encourage members to participate, they are given Kshs 3,000, lunch and a snack. During the monthly forum, attendees are given Kshs 200. The Cooperative started a milk processing factory which produces Fresha Milk products in 2004.

The cooperative has adapted to the changes of the time. For example, it has worked strategies for incorporating women as shareholders in the cooperative and also including other members of the family if need be. This is done to reduce conflicts. It began with the realisation that women could monetise their daily production activities on the family farm. They also realised working on the farm generated more money than *kibarua* (casual labour). They were also advantaged by the fact that training was also available. The cooperative also encouraged women participation in economic activities by supplying groceries in their stores. This reduced the time that women spent on farming food, harvesting, cleaning and cooking, and gave them time to concentrate on dairy farming.

Githunguri Dairy Farmers' Cooperative in Kiambu County has embedded modernity and capitalism in its institutions. If a man dies, the wife takes over the shareholding, and later transfers it to the children. Some families do transfer shares to their daughters. Adulterating of milk attracts a fine of Kshs 20,000 or expulsion from the cooperative. Lateness or absence from meetings without a valid reason also attracts a penalty.

The amalgamation of several households into the Githunguri Dairy Cooperative harnesses agency for its evolution. The cooperative is over fifty years old. Githunguri Dairy Cooperative Society (which deals with milk production, processing and marketing) model is resilient and successful. It creates jobs, alleviates poverty, is self-managed, independent and inclusive in terms of gender and youth. It has succeeded where other agricultural-based cooperatives in the region have not performed well (Kinyanjui 2002). The Githunguri Dairy Cooperative is a complex case of adaption and articulation of a commodity to global development. The cooperative has initiated institutions that benefit the local peasants and ensure that the effects of extraction and exploitation are reduced.

Githunguri Dairy and Cooperative movement has contributed to the enhancement of wealth and wellbeing in the community. It has contributed towards the construction of schools, churches and health centres in the area. It has incorporated its members into health insurance schemes such as the National Hospital Insurance Fund (NHIF). Through its 'Store' initiative, members can access foodstuff for their households on credit and repay through a monthly check-off system. Members can also access farm inputs on credit and repay on a monthly or quarterly basis through the check-off system. Women can therefore manage the "dry period" and are freed from daily food production efforts to pay greater attention to livestock management. Households make biogas from cow dung and the energy produced is used for cooking, heating and lighting. Food production in the farm is also enhanced by supply of manure. Thus, reproduction, production and exchange are integrated into the household and addresses some of the feminine challenges that hinder women from participating in production. It has created a system of production and exchange that is sustainable and generates wealth and wellbeing for the people. Members are provided with loans to buy motorbikes which they use fetch animal feeds from distant places or deliver milk to the collecting centre. Youth are making carts for delivering milk, repairing milk carts or working as factory operatives in the milk production, feeds, metal work, construction and auxiliary industries.

The result is that income inequality has reduced substantially as most households participate in dairy farming. Parents and adult children are included in the family SACCO account for ease of transactions and guaranteeing of loans. The area was ranked the second safest constituency in 2015 in the Kiambu County Report. (Kiambu County Report, 2015). The model has been widely embraced by the youth. The youth are employed in the factory, or in dairy farming support services such as transport, feed and farm tools production. There is intensive training for members. This is done in a participatory manner. Any innovations introduced are approved by the membership. Procured veterinary officers are fully qualified and competent. They are vetted by the board and the members. Companies willing to partner or do business with the cooperative also undergo rigorous vetting. Service providers have to offer samples of their products free of charge to a minimum of ten farmers in each of the nine milk collection routes. The ensuing feedback determines whether the service provider can do business with the cooperative.

In this book, conversations were held with three women to illustrate how they are articulating their logic and solidarities to adapt to this form of production.

Gatukuyu Coffee Growers Cooperative

Coffee was introduced to peasants to extract their labour to serve the interests of global coffee consumption. The small scale coffee farmers were organised into cooperatives for ease of management of the extraction process. The cooperatives educated farmers and organised the first stage processing of coffee before sale in coffee auctions. In the 1970s and 1980s, the cooperative was very strong and had a membership of close to 25,000 households (Kinyanjui, 2002). Over time, the membership declined due to farmers'resistance to extraction and exploitation by marketers at the local and global level. The first resistance was in 1976 after some farmers visited the London Coffee Auction. The farmers realised that there was a lot of exploitation in the coffee trade and demanded to break away from the Kiambu Farmers' Union whom they identified as the first line of exploitation (Kinyanjui, 2002). The second wave of resistance in the 1990s was occasioned by the fall of the global coffee commodity prices and the structural adjustment–generated coffee reforms. This resistance which targeted the local cooperative leadership was marked by violence that was brutally stopped by the government (Kinyanjui, 2002). Many farmers abandoned coffee farming making most of the factories to operate below capacity.

Some farmers still continue with production under the Gatukuyu Farmers' Cooperative. After the death of the first generation of cooperators, their wives took over their cooperative membership. They have joined the bandwagon of extraction and exploitation through coffee production and exchange. This book illustrates how these women are articulating their logic and solidarities in coffee production for livelihood survival.

This chapter has described the activities in which Wanjiku, engages in livelihood survival. In the Githunguri and Gatukuyu cooperatives livelihood survival activities, products were introduced to local peasants to extract and exploit their labour to meet the needs of local and global consumption. In the rest of the survival activities-Kimalel Goat Auction, Kisii Soap Stone, Kakamega Soghum Traders, Kienyeji Chicken farmers, and Usare Beach Fish Traders, the local communities articulate indigenous commodities like fish, sorghum, soapstone, goats, chicken and land to global production and consumption. In Kamukunji, the artisans use their labour and skills to adapt to global production. In all these cases women are involved and use their logic and solidarities to navigate through these activities for their survival and that of their offspring. The next chapter will demonstrate how Wanjiku's logic, self-determination and self-reliance leads to her articulation in production and exchange.

CHAPTER SIX

WANJIKU'S LOGIC OF PARTICIPATION IN PEASANT, ARTISAN AND TRADE ACTIVITIES

This chapter describes Wanjiku's logic in global development through peasant, artisan and trade activities. It shows how she has managed to monetise production and exchange in her livelihood activities. It documents the strategies and methods that she uses to enter into money circuits of production and exchange. She has articulated her products (such as chicken, milk and sorghum) which she uses for reproduction and nurturing into global development. She follows her husband in fishing, goat auction and artisan work. She constructs extra rooms in her compound at home, making the household a site for capital generation and circulation. By articulating these activities in global production, she is able to connect production with reproduction, consumption, nurturing, wealth and well-being. Production and exchange are embedded in personal, community and divine realms of her daily life. The underlying factors of entry into monetisation, capital formation and circulation ensure human survival and thriving families and communities. Capital formation is influenced by the logic of nurturing, connecting community, as well as creating community for harnessing individual and group agency.

Here is Harvey's (2010) pp 40-41 definition of capital:

> "Capital is not a thing but a process in which money is perpetually sent in search of more money. Capitalists – those who set this process in motion – take on many different personae. Finance capitalists look to make more money by lending to others in return for interest. Merchant capitalists buy cheap and sell dear. Landlords collect rent because the land and properties they own are scarce resources. Renters make money from royalties and intellectual property rights. Asset traders swap titles (to stocks and shares for example), debts and contracts (including insurance) for a profit. Even the state can act like a capitalist, as, for example, when it uses tax revenues to invest in infrastructures that stimulate growth and generate even more tax revenues.

> But the form of capital circulation that has come to dominate from the mid-eighteenth century onwards is that of industrial or production

capital. In this case the capitalist starts the day with a certain amount of money, and, having selected a technology and organisational form, goes into the market place and buys the requisite amounts of labour power and means of production (raw materials, physical plant, intermediate products, machinery, energy and the like). The labour power is combined with the means of production through an active labour process conducted under the supervision of the capitalist. The result is a commodity that is sold by its owner, the capitalist, in the market place for a profit."

In the above paragraphs, Harvey (2010) presents scenarios on how individuals enter into capitalism. Money is key in the process. One has to have a commodity such as land to exchange for money. Money is used to generate more money. The individual, a capitalist, sells a commodity in the market for profit.

The Beijing conference of 1995 ratified that poverty is feminised (UN, 1995). To arrest poverty, the Women and Girl Effect was initiated to address the feminisation of poverty in the Beijing platform. Focus was placed on women and girl's education, financial inclusion, health and effects of conflict on women. Feminisation of poverty can only be addressed if the activities and socio-economic transactions of women are given monetary value in a fair and just manner.

Peasant studies define the African society's mode of production and demonstrate how the African peasantry became incorporated into the money economy. Ochonu (2013) observes that the African mode of production was based on a traditional logic of subsistence and could not be related to the market-oriented production of Europe.

Immanuel Wallerstein (1974, 1980, 1989) traces Africa's entry into the global economy to the Atlantic slave trade and the introduction of agricultural commodity production. Wallerstein also observes that colonialism opened up Africa to the world economy through the development of transport infrastructure such as the Kenya Uganda railway that linked the hinterland to the Mombasa port; establishment of marketing boards; and introduction of new crops and animals for European markets.

Ochonu (2013) notes that the introduction of colonial measures of value, mainly currency, and the outlawing of pre-colonial standards of value and currency like manila, cowry shells, metal bars, cloth, etc. served several ends. Colonial authorities used it to enforce the payment of taxes in early colonial days when many conquered

African groups were struggling to adjust to the unfamiliar routine of taxation. Tax payment was a compulsory obligation to the colonial government and evasion attracted severe punishment, and because taxes could only be paid in the colonial currency, Africans had no choice but to enter into one or multiple sectors of the colonial economy as a way to earn the colonial currency. The introduction of colonial currencies compelled Africans to become labourers on European-owned colonial enterprises, become peasant, market-oriented producers and entrenched tax payment. Africans were compelled to make purchases of essential goods with colonial monetary units (Ochonu, 2013: 8).

The Postcolonial State and the Peasantry

After independence many African governments crafted policies to transform traditional productions processes. Almost all African governments established ministries of agriculture to educate farmers through extension services and demonstration farms such as Waruhiu Farm in Kiambu and Wambugu Farm in Nyeri Kenya. Farmers would visit these farms to be trained on good crop and animal farming. Agricultural shows allowed farmers to showcase their products, compete for markets and exchange ideas. The shows were held in all the provincial (and later district) headquarters. Through the Kenya Agricultural Research Institute, Coffee Research Institute, the Tea Research Institute, the Potato Research Institute and ILRI, exotic breeds, seeds and plant varieties were developed and introduced to farmers through farmer training programmes or government extension services. Boards for coffee, tea, pyrethrum, sugar and cotton were created to facilitate marketing of products. Today, some of these boards have collapsed or have been restructured. They have large operating costs which eat into farmers' output (Kinyanjui, 2013) and deny the farmers agency to market their products. Associations like the Kenya Farmers' Association have been interfered with and weakened by politics (Kinyanjui, 2002). They frustrate a majority of small-scale farmers and lead them to bondage.

There is no definite agenda to realise monetisation and the multiplication of money in an unequal world. The world is unequal in terms of technology development and evolution of capitalism. Capitalism, as practised today, thrives through the exploitation of some communities by others. Although there are many studies on the intensity and nature of poverty and desire to eradicate it, in most instances development practitioners efforts have not always been successful. Large scale projects have been abandoned after huge investments. Peasants, traders and artisans are intriguing in the sense that they get by, don't romanticise poverty, and create options for negotiating livelihood based on human intuition. Humanness and human intuition as a strategy is considered unscientific but it is the most important thing Africa can offer the world (Dowden, 2010 and Tutu,1999).

Logic for Entry

Inadvertently, Wanjiku through her reproductive and production role plays a vital role in ensuring human survival as well as thriving families and communities in the country. Human survival is contingent upon the extension of the family tree. To realise this goal, women provide basic needs such as food, water, health and education. Women contribute to thriving families and communities by maintaining interdependent relationships between individuals. The relationships are maintained through distribution of resources, sharing and reciprocity.

Wanjiku engages in reproduction, production and consumption by constructing a household economy whose transaction is based on principles of self-reliance, resilience, persistence, sustainability, sharing, reciprocity and solidarity. Her logic of participation in the household economy is to ensure survival and concomitant thriving families and communities. Most of the social and economic activities that ensure human survival and thriving communities are closely tied to the household. The household is not only a space for nurturing and caring, it is also a space for work, production, exchange and consumption where socio-economic activities are constructed around the household. Even with the onset of colonialism, women traded in crops, grown on the family farm. They made clothes from animal skin or fibre obtained from the neighbourhood forests. Utensils were made from pottery pits in community neighbourhood or from vegetable matter grown on the farm. To intensify production, women would band together to perform rotational tasks for different households. The women were key in the management of the household socio-economic activities and connecting families and communities.

With the advent of colonialism, Wanjiku lost her means of reproduction, production and consumption in the household. Her centre of production, exchange and consumption was disrupted as expressed in the song *Mbia Ciokire.*

Perhaps one of the greatest losses to Wanjiku was the loss of the homestead granary. New seed crops, technologies, restrictions on clearing of new grounds or virgin land for farming after gazetting of forests had a heavy toll on women's control in food production. It is no wonder that in the song, the woman is thrown past the granary.

New food crops like rice were also introduced. The popular child play song: *mūcree nī mwega nī ūrīagwo na gīciko riria ngutua kūria nengereria gīciko (*rice is good. When I want to eat rice, give me a spoon) acculturated communities into accepting rice as a staple food in homes. The local shopkeeper, rather than the granary, became the supplier of clothing and food. Wheat, pasta, bread, cabbage and *sukuma wiki* replaced indigenous vegetables such as *managu, thabai*, and *terere.* Wanjiku had to respond to this change in foods by engaging in trade to provide for the household. Education at the household was taken over by schools and also became a commercial activity. Health was also commoditized outside the home.

As mentioned earlier, men were the first to gain entry into the monetised economy. They were captured and conscripted to work in mines, plantations, police forces, ports or in the transport sector. They were also recruited to work as houseboys and domestic security workers. They transferred money to their wives in rural areas since women migration into cities was controlled (Kinyanjui, 2014). Majority of the women were late comers in monetised production and exchange yet they were still charged with the responsibility of ensuring survival and thriving families and communities. The women gradually realised that they had to articulate their production and exchange into the monetised economy. Most women traders, artisans, peasants and fisherfolk state that their logic of entry into monetised production and exchange was to provide food for the family as well as cater for their everyday needs such as clothing, housing, health and schooling. Underlying this logic is the fact that some of the activities like education of children which women used to perform in the household were taken away from them.

Wanjiku's logic is largely geared towards human survival as well as thriving families and communities. Human survival is largely dependent on food, good health and education. She therefore celebrates her ability to buy foodstuff. For example, Grace Achieng reports that her participation in the fish trade enables her to buy food. Peris Kibet says that she is able to provide food for the family through the auction of goats. Provision of basic needs for the family was frequently mentioned as a logic for entry into monetised economy. Grace Achieng, Lilian Ochieng, Lilian Onyango, Rehema Ongwen, Christine Lewatachum, Susan Kegongo, Fransisca Atsango and Agnes Masitsa all observe that they joined the monetised economy to be able to meet the basic needs of their families.

According to Grace Ochieng, 'this trade has really uplifted the standard of living for my family considering that my background is very poor. I can now meet my needs. When I get profit, I draw a budget and plough back part of the money into the business, paying of school fees for my children and family upkeep. I am now able to provide for my family with ease."

Participation in fishing allows the women involved to take up responsibilities that were hitherto for men. A good example is building a homestead, which was the work of men. Lilian Onyago states that through her business, she has been able to build two houses, one for herself and the other one for her mother. She has also diversified her business activities by engaging in chicken rearing.

"From this business, I have built a house for my mother. I bought her seats, foodstuff and catered for her medical expenses. I am also paying school fees for my children."

Rehema Ongwen shares similar sentiments. She says that from fishing, "I am paying school fees for my children who presently are in universities."

The same applies to Christine Lewatachum who says, "I am paying school fees for my children who are studying in universities from the money I earn from the goat auction. I save the balance with the Kenya Commercial Bank. In this way, I am building my capital base. I have also diversified my business activities by buying parcels of land and planting napier grass for sale."

Peris Kibet indicates that she joined the Kimalel Goat Auction to enable her pay school fees for her children and donate towards church development. She has also been able to engage in honey processing and has purchased two parcels of land which she is planning to develop. Being in possession of money has positively boosted her social status in the community. Susan Kegongo's proceeds from goat auction have helped her pay school fees as well as meet her house rent levies. Agnes Masitsa observes that having money has enabled her to assist her mother who is a widow, pay house rent and also support the needy in the community. Anna Jane from Githunguri discerns that the proceeds from selling milk to Githunguri Dairy Cooperative have helped her educate her children while Jane Mwangi of Gatukuyu Coffee Growers Cooperative has used her earnings from coffee to bring up and educate her children. Felista Muthoni and Njeri Njoroge also express that engagement in coffee farming has helped them bring up their children. Janet Gitonga, Rose Kamani and Mary Kivuva who are engaged in Kienyeji chicken farming observe that they have been able to bring up their children using the earnings from chicken sales.

The above responses demonstrate that women's entry in the money culture helps them fulfill personal, family and community roles. They align their logic of entry into global development with production, reproduction and consumption. They are able to meet their reproductive role by farming, trade and artisan activities. This has largely happened because of their need for self-reliance and determination to see their household survive and thrive. Once these roles are met, they diversify their business activities to other activities like chicken rearing, honey processing and purchasing plots. They are moving towards having tangible capital. Land parcels are a foundation for wealth as are incomes through farming, building rental houses, or speculation. The women are able to harness key factors of production which are likely to deepen their position in the capitalist global economy. They have rights to property which they did not have prior to participating in economic activities such as fishing, goat auction, artisan, or peasant activities.

Production and Distribution

Many scholars like Hart (1973) and Chen (2012) argue that African traders, artisans, peasants and fishing communities are trapped in precarious family and neighbourhood networks. They state that participation in economic informality is the cause of their poverty. Getting out of these precarious activities is the pathway to development, poverty alleviation and job creation. This will set the stage for creating individuality and freedom in society which is the beginning of entrepreneurship, creativity and innovation.

While this sounds plausible, the flipside of solidarity, family and neighbourhood networks have not been explored in terms of the relationship and distribution of income among members of those networks. Sharing and reciprocity are part of the distributive mechanism in family and neighbourhood networks. Sharing, gifting and reciprocity advance human survival in the family, continuity into the next generation and guarantee income for individual family members who have no direct access to income. This overrides the feeling that the family and neighbourhood networks create dependency and encourage laziness.

Women have an important role of connecting people, communities and generations. By so doing they contribute to income distribution in the family and neighbourhood networks. The distribution of income takes place in monetary terms or in kind where everyday practical needs of human survival are met and facilitation of family and community is done. The distributive mechanisms associated with women traders, artisans, peasants and fisherfolk are often viewed as wasteful. It is for this reason that Hyden (1983) proposes that economies of affection have to be dealt with for progress to be realised. The reliance on endowed relatives by other family or neighbourhood members has been critical in the distribution of resources and providing a stepping stone for the advancement of other siblings in the family or members of the community. In most cases, members feel obliged to engage in resource distribution through sharing or reciprocal arrangements.

*****

Building the community is also an important logic for women's participation in global development through trade, peasant and artisan work. They share their resources with members of the extended family, especially parents. Most of the women feel that ensuring the welfare of their family members through sharing of resources is an important logic for their engagement in business. They distribute or share their income with family members as a matter of obligation or as a reciprocation for generosity from others, especially to mothers. This care work largely goes on unpaid and women do not expect to be paid. A recipient of support today would aid someone else on another day. According to custom, a person who was cared for, by the mother, for example, would name her girl child after the mother. This was considered to be a form of reciprocation or paying the person who brought her up.

Women earnings in trade, craft, fishing and peasant activities are thus used in support of parents or siblings. Some build houses for their parents, pay for their medical needs or provide for their daily upkeep in form of food. The complexity of women participation in monetised production is both productive and distributive. It is distributive in the sense that it supports those who are young and not old enough to engage in production, those who are aged and can no longer provide for themselves and those who are out of productive work. All this is geared to establish harmony in the household and ensure its thriving and flourishing.

Everyone is guaranteed survival even without income. This is expressed when Lilian Onyango says that, "my participation in fish trade has greatly improved my relationship with my mother. I take care of her and we share a lot. She gives me advice on how to succeed in this trade on things to do and things not to do. For the case of my husband, we are living in harmony because we are able to cater for each other's needs and wants."

Similar sentiments on distribution of income to those who do not have are expressed by Rhoda that, "I assist in paying school fees for my brother's kids who passed on long time ago."

Distribution of income among family members is also expressed by Nancy Juma, "the money I generate from the sorghum farming helps me to take care of my family."

Lilian Onyango celebrates her entry into trade because she is able to take care of her parents. She is able to take care of her mother who is sick by buying her expensive medication. Rhoda celebrates her success for being able to take her children and brothers to school. She is also able to buy a cow for her parents. She has been a source of income for her large family. She observes that from the business, she is able to pay the school fees for her two children and brothers. She hails from a polygamous family where her father had 12 wives. He did this because he was born alone and wanted to have a large family. The logic of having offspring and the complexity of siblings supporting each other enhances human survival and continuity to the next generation. It also allows the redistribution of income in the family and community.

*****

Enhancing a woman's status in the community is also another reason for logic of entry. Women leadership in the community is reflected in the ability to help other women solve household problems. These problems range from children's discipline, marital conflicts or domestic violence. Christine Lewatuchum has boosted her profile in society as a problem solver in marital issues. She says: "I have assisted many women in their marriages and try to reduce domestic violence."

Rehema Ongwen says that her participation in trade has enhanced her position in leadership among other women. "I can be in a position to advice people on this kind of business because I know the merits and demerits," she says. Similar sentiments are expressed by Fransisca Atsango who observes that she has become a good advisor to women who want to venture into sustainable business.

*****

By participating in peasant, artisan and trade activities, women are able to adapt and meet changing demands. They are able to provide housing for themselves and their families. While traditionally women were provided with housing first by parents and then by husbands, the dynamics have now changed. First there are single women who have to provide housing for themselves and their children. Increased women migration into towns has also forced them to seek housing where they pay rent or build their own.

"It's from sorghum farming that I am living in town and pay rent," says Nancy Juma.

Jacinta also expresses the following: "From artisan work, I have built a house in Kahawa West and my rural home. I have brick houses from this business."

Concomitant with the desire to provide for housing is the logic of buying land. In most African communities, women accessed land through their husbands. In central Kenya one of the ways people got introduced into the capitalist mode of production was through the Swynnerton plan in which commoditized land and gave titles to men in the 1950s (Thurston, 1987). This gave men authority over family land. They could sell and dispose or grow cash crops on it for money. As women play catch up with men, they are also investing in land or plots in the city and other urban centres.

Jacinta observes the following: "I have bought pieces land and built rental houses."

As mentioned earlier, the woman's role of educating children at the fireside was taken away from her and education commoditized. Women perpetuate their role in the education of their children by using their earnings to take them to school.

"I am so happy to be able to pay school fees for my children," says a jubilant Fransisca Atsango. Nancy Juma similarly remarks that, "from sorghum farming, my children are going to school. I pay school fees for my children who study at the university."

*****

Scholars of African religion describe Africans as being notoriously religious. Traditionally, women did not contribute goats or other animals for sacrifice. Since appeasing the gods has become a commercial activity and offerings in the form of money is an important part of Christian worship, women are now part of the process. That is why Anne Jane in Githunguri states that one of the reasons for her engagement in monetised production is to stop begging for church offerings from her husband. She has joined the cadre of women who are active in the church through giving tithes and various types of offerings. It is also a way of thanking God for making their businesses to be successful.

As Rhoda and Jacinta observe separately, "I have seen a lot of blessing from the tithes and offerings I give to the church."

Financial Inclusion and Assets

It is widely held that lack of finance stymies national development, growth of businesses and improvement of standards of living for a large number of people in the developing world. Many studies have interrogated the issue of finance in households, business, and schools, among other areas. Lack of finance is used as an explanation variable for chronic poverty. Johnson (2004) examines the nature of financial landscape in Karatina town. She documents the different financial platforms and institutions which ordinary people use in Karatina and evaluates the financial landscape with the hope of improving micro financing in Kenya. She concludes that the microfinance sector is not competitive enough and has not penetrated the local financial market. In other studies based on FSD financial surveys, in Kenya and Uganda Johnson (2004) proposes the policy needs to address social and demographic factors that affect individuals' access to finance.

Ferrand (1999) is a PhD study that is based on the concept of the 'missing middle' in the Kenya Industrial structure. Ferrrand argues that the Kenya industrial structure is dominated by many micro and small firms at the bottom, few middle-sized firms and a good supply of large firms. The development agenda, therefore, should address the issue of the missing middle and provide solutions. It has been argued that increasing the number of middle-sized firms would be good for the economy because they would create more jobs. Ferrand argues that firms fail to evolve from small to middle because of lack of finance and recommends financial sector deepening that is funded by donors to support and extend financial inclusion as well as regulation of SACCOs, among others.

In my study, Kinyanjui (1992) among small and medium sized firms in Central Kenya interrogates the source of finances and how finances impact on firms' performance. In the paper on finance and availability of capital in the *Journal of East African Development Research*, I observed that most of the firms were founded through own savings, SACCOs, credit organisations and government programmes. Revisiting the idea of finance again in Kinyanjui (2012), I argue that *vyama* or *chama* are an important instrument used by ordinary people to coordinate markets and organise society. I argue that the *vyama* concept evolved from an African cultural institution which among the Gikuyu was *Ngwatio,* or *Matega*. It operates on the principle of pooling resources, gifting, solidarity and reciprocity. Through *vyama*, people have bought plots and financed household transactions. *Vyama* are indeed an institution of hope which create a community for enhancing individual and group agency for collective action to surmount socio-economic action.

Financial inclusion and asset portfolio became a development issues in the 1990s (Ferrand 2013) One popular argument propounded by neoliberal development scholars is with regard to availability, access of finance to women asset ownership. Many development financial scholars and activists bemoan the failure of banking institutions to avail capital finance to women. Others argue that women do not have tangible assets to serve as collateral. Nobel laureate Muhamud Yunus provided the saving grace for providing finance to the poor. He developed the Grameen Microfinance Model that provided small loans to women without collateral (Khandker et al, 1994). In the model, women would get into a group for purposes of borrowing based on the principle that the women in the group would guarantee each other. This provided women with cash to invest in business and cater for their other transactions. Yunus' effort was lauded globally and was accepted as a strategy for financing the poor. The World Bank and most of the Third World, including Africa and Latin America quickly adopted this model that Roy (2010) refers to as Poverty Capital. Provision of microfinance was propagated on the basis of poverty alleviation and economic empowerment. In spite of the many philanthropist groups, donor agencies and non-governmental organisations and government initiating microfinance programmes, lack financial inclusion for a large number of people still looms large. A model that will fully solve the issue is yet to be developed.

In order to dig deeper into the issue of financial inclusion, this book examines the logic and process of monetisation of women peasants, traders and artisans. This chapter addresses the processes and logic of monetisation among women peasants, traders, artisans and how they organise their money circulation as well as accumulation of assets.

Anne Jane from Githunguri says that the inception of women into monetisation through dairy farming began with their local women neighbourhood groups. They would pool money and give it to one woman who would buy a calf. The woman would then nurture the calf till it was ready for milking. This process requires a lot of patience and solidarity among the women. They prefer this method rather than going for microfinancing because of the microfinance repayment problem. For example, one can obtain a microfinance loan to buy a calf and then it dies. The lender will not wait until the calf starts to provide milk for sale to start claiming its due. Further, if one defaults, household goods are auctioned. In their own arrangement, if the calf dies, the women come again in solidarity and bail each other out just as they do it in the case of funerals, illness or death. Anne Jane also says that microfinance, although based on a group concept, encourages individualism and vengeance rather than the local women group whose philosophy is based on gifting, solidarity, sharing, reciprocity, self-reliance and self-actualisation rather than engagement in arrangements that leave one extremely indebted. This philosophy is contrary to neoliberal economic sense which believes in leapfrogging businesses through introduction of large volumes of capital and technology. The peasants believe in a slow but sure approach. It is based on the natural processes of the rising up, sowing of seeds in the ground, waiting for them to germinate, grow and then dry, and harvest. It also influenced by the local orature of success and failure. For example, one story has it that a woman who could not pay her debt shunned her family and neighbourhood to hide from the microfinance officers. Other narratives attributed microfinance cash to money from the devil and demanded human sacrifice for one to succeed.

The women also prefer tangible assets rather than paper money. Asset buying and investing in a cause rather than saving in a bank is also another way of 'hiding money' or locally 'storing money in holes.' Rodah buys a piece of land for herself and livestock for her parents. Jacinta Wanjiru aka Mama Kamukunji invests in her childrens' learning, purchases parcels of land, purchases a car for personal use and hire, constructs rental houses, and services domestic family needs.

From Jacinta we can observe a variety of activities which include gifting, reciprocity, diverse methods of deploying surplus, meeting personal needs, improving mobility, connecting family, and investing in the next generation. A neoliberal approach would emphasise reinvesting in the same business so that it can grow, improving technology and innovations to upgrade business rather than diversifying the household portfolio. Grace Achieng also illustrates the slow but sure approach to engage in business.

She observes that, "I started this business in early 2013 because of the poverty level in my family. I started selling fish worth Kshs 2,000 and generated a profit of Kshs 1,000."

While neoliberal approaches bemoan the lack of risk taking of many traders, artisans and peasants, it is important to understand the logic behind their approaches. They are based on processes of socialisation built on trust or other familiar relationships which determine how the businesses should be run.

For example, Lilian Anyango says, "my mum introduced me to the fish trade in 2013. She no longer does this business because she is very sick and I am the one who is supporting her. One has to hang in there."

Christine Lewachum who is 49 years old is a single parent. She resides at Kisiwa in Baringo but moved to Kailel due to insecurity in her area. She started selling goats in 2015. One could argue that alimony and child support, or giving man a fish through cash transfer could help alleviate the predicament of these two women. Why should we deny them the ability to use their creative agency to sustain themselves? Participation in peasant, artisan and trade activities enhances the pride of doing something for oneself rather than becoming dependant on someone else.

The following testimonies also indicate the diversity of issues involved in the entry into businesses. They all point to forming businesses based on a form of humanism. Susan Kengogo started her business of selling honey in 2011 which she bought at Kshs 4,200 and sold at Kshs.10,000. She has grown her business from this humble start up.

Agnes Masitsa also used the same route, "I started this business in May 1999, after being laid off as a sales lady in a bakery firm called Kabras Millers. The money they gave me as compensation, I decided to put all in to the business. At first I bought 7 sacks of maize. From the profits, I added beans, millet, groundnuts, *ndengu*, simsim, cassava and sorghum." She applies her creative agency to flourish.

Anne Wanjiku Kionga demonstrates the use of creative agency in the monetisation project. "I was introduced to this business by my husband. He was a civil servant and had a stall. Since I was a housewife and didn't have anything to do, I decided to help him. This was way back in 1995," She testifies.

Beatrice Achieng uses her creative agency to engage in trade rather than being dependant on her husband, "I started this business in 2006 immediately after being married. Initially, I was a tailor and my husband used to do this business alone. He then introduced me to it and left me to continue with it. Gradually, I learnt the business and mastered it. I started with a few two kilogrammes of cereals. After selling and getting profit, I re-invested the money back into the business. After stocking enough kilos of cereals including sorghum, I knew I was ready to become a wholesaler."

Fransisca Atsango also used her creative agency to achieve her goals. "I started this business in 1998 as a retailer and gradually became a wholesaler. At the time, a majority of the current wholesalers were retailers. However, loans from the Kenya Women Finance Trust (KWFT) propelled them to become wholesalers. As the number of wholesalers increased, business started dwindling and led to loan defaults. I was not affected since I had not procured a loan from KWFT. I started this business with only 40 kilogrammes of millet. Gradually, I saved and re-invested back the profits into the business till I became a wholesaler."

Nancy Juma combined her use of creative agency with scheduled growth that fitted into her way of life. "I started this business in 1993 with only 2 kilogrammes of maize and beans. Gradually, I increased my stock to 5 kilogrammes, 10 kilogrammes, until I started dealing with sacks. As my stock increased, I added more cereals to my stock to include; millet, cassava and sorghum," she says.

Rodha, like the other women, uses her creative agency, desire for self-reliance and the need to build herself in her monetisation process. "At first I came visiting my sister living in Nairobi, then decided to look for job. I was employed with the National Cereals and Produce Board (NCPB) for two weeks. Afterwards, I was laid off. My sister was among the pioneers of Kamukunji Jua Kali. By then, there were only three women namely, 'Bibi ya Njunguna', 'Bibi ya Kamotho', and the late Monicah. It is estimated that there were 370 registered traders that time. After looking for job and staying with my sister and family for two years, I opted to move out and stay alone. My sister encouraged me and gave me Kshs1,000. I had extra money and used the sum to make one set of large, medium and small *masanduku* (boxes). From the profit garnered from the sales, I made more boxes and invited my two brothers to join me."

Jacinta Wanjiru, aka Mama Kamukunji, utilises creative agency and takes calculated risks as part of her strategy to stay in her lifelong business. She has limited options for failure. This means that she has to hang in there amidst all odds. "I started this business in1978. Initially, this place was not as congested as today and the grass was very tall. Before starting this job, I used to be a tailor at Uhuru market. I would make clothes and distribute them to other towns. Since the venture was not profitable, I decided to try my luck in artisan work in Kamukunji. In Kamukunji, we were only three of us at the time: Ngugi, Gachagua and I. I started with only one drum. One drum would cost Kshs 5 and I would sell it at Kshs15. Before shifting to the present stall where I am now selling metal sheets and scrap metals, my first location was the famous Nyayo sheds. I borrowed some money from a friend and increased my stock from one drum to five drums which I would sell at buying at Kshs 20. There was a high demand for drums then. I would sell up to 100 drums in a month. I would even sell drums to outside markets like Uganda. When I heard that President Moi would allocate stalls to skilled artisans, I learnt how to make cooking stoves and be more proficient in metal box manufacture. Only two women were engaged in this activity, the late Mama Wangora and I. That's how I secured Stall No. 19 where I make cooking stoves, pots, wheelbarrows and boxes. I have entrusted the business to my children due to my advanced age."

Peris Kibet used the same route of creative agency to monetisation. "During President Moi's era," she says. "I was selling honey. I used to buy honey from honey fetchers, process and package it, then sell it. I used the money obtained to buy and rear goats in 2014, as well as grow tomatoes under the Molok irrigation scheme."

This kind of humanistic model of business makes us question the ideal of leapfrogging businesses through technical fixes. It needs understanding the logic, norms and values that are held by traders, artisans and peasants. The trajectory of women inclusion in circuits of money as illustrated by these case studies may not lead to fetching more money in the Harvey (2010) sense. Their entry into money is interlinked with personal, family and community dimensions. It is also connected to lived experience. The money fetched (however little) is used to meet specific personal, human and community needs. Neoliberal approaches would see this as failed entrepreneurship, limited vision and lack of enabling environment in terms of access to marketing, finance, and technology. The humanism business model which combines gifting, reciprocity, nurturing, individual, group agency, insurgency, extending and family thriving into the next generation affects and complicates the scenario of management and operations of peasants, artisans and traders economy is a fundamental challenge to development practitioners and financers who want to leapfrog peasants, artisans and traders into neoliberal economic models. There is need to restructure our methodologies and rethink our philosophies of change.

Archie Mafeje (1991) argues that development knowledge should be rooted in the local African experience. The chapter has shown Wanjiku's desire to reclaim what colonialism took away from her. She has articulated her commodities, labour and resources to global development and at the same time maintained her logic of reproduction, production and consumption. She has adapted to the changing realities in her own terms by resisting micro-finance indebtedness and preferring to use her *chama* and gradual growth of business. She has maintained the social organisation of her household, extended family and community. Slowly she is bridging the gap of separating production, reproduction and consumption that was introduced during colonialism. In the next chapter we demonstrate how she has made efforts to articulate her business model.

CHAPTER SEVEN

TOWARDS WANJIKU'S BUSINESS MODEL

Most scholars view globalisation and capitalism as bad for women. Scholars such as JK Gibson-Graham (2006) see the end of capitalism as the solution to global development inequalities. In the early 19th century, some scholars viewed socialist policies as being more favourable than capitalism in liberating women from work. Empirical studies on women workers in global firms depict them as oppressed and denied human rights in production and exchange Opondo (2005). Care activities, a major preoccupation of women, are not considered part of the global production Ravazi (2009). Most of the scholars recommend inclusion of women in financial circuits through neoliberal and capitalist credit frameworks. They rarely address the logic and process of women monetisation and reactions towards the culture of money. They also do not acknowledge the displacement and dislocation of women experience in the household due to their entry into the capitalist neoliberal framework.

Arguably, scholars investigating women's entry into the culture of money posit a situation where women monetisation takes place through a different path from that of men. For example, White (1980) in her book *The Comfort of Home* demonstrates that women migrants in Nairobi entered the new colonial economy through prostitution and those who were more enterprising were able to build businesses from earnings generated from the trade. Claire Robertson (1997), analysing women's entry into bean trade in Nairobi showed that it was an escape route from problems and troubles in their homes. Other scholars Mwatha-Karega (1997) have argued that women join businesses through a gendered vehicle locally referred to as *chama*. She argues that women move from welfare activities into small income generating activities where they are innovative, take risks, invest and reinvest accumulated capital through their enterprises. Other studies argue that women's businesses do not grow or remain the same because they are undercapitalised (Mwatha-Karega, 1997). Nomsa Daniels observes that financial exclusion of women is a global problem with 'more than 1.3 billion women in the world operating outside the formal financial system' (Demirguc-Kunt, Klapper & Singer, 2017:2). This situation is mirrored in Africa where more than 70 percent of women are reportedly financially excluded and their access to finance and financial services is consistently behind that of their male counterparts (Johnson, 2004).

Accelerating women's financial inclusion thus requires bold and sustained action to advance women's economic opportunities and rights, and to ensure that they can meaningfully participate in the economy without undue constraints and barriers that limit their progress. New strategies of financial inclusion such as Mpesa and Sportpesa advertisements target women, assuring them of freedom from financial constraints. These advertisement gimmicks are intended to draw women into global capitalist financial models which are extractive and exploitative.

While women have been trying to gain entry into monetised global production and exchange, they tend to construct a business model that resonates with their experiences and is not exploitative as expressed in the song *Mbia Ciokire*. There is strong oral tradition and popular culture that critic women entry into the neoliberal frame of production and exchange as well as engagement in extractive and exploitative businesses.Women who engage in businesses that combine production and reproduction are praised.

Women have been struggling to recover and take back their position in the economy through solidarity entrepreneurialism (Kinyanjui, 2012, 2013, 2014). Solidarity entrepreneurialism is akin to the third way of dealing with social justice proposed by Archbishop Desmond Tutu of South Africa. According to Tutu (1999), the third way uses *Ubuntu* (solidarity and humanness) which is based on the principle that human beings are inextricably bound to each other. Women, peasants, artisans and market traders have embraced the *Utu-Ubuntu* business model in carrying out their businesses. This is captured by the sample stories from the women interviewed. They have been trying to re-embed the personal, the community and the divine in the evolution of a business model. Competition and individual interests exist but within the context of solidarity. In the market, traders selling similar products will set prices in a manner that does not antagonise their fellow traders. In Gikomba, the second-hand clothes market, traders have evolved a blind auction which they refer to as `camera` for selling shoes and garments. In the camera system, a person offers a price for the good shirts in a bale before opening it. The person with the highest bid will be the first to select. The process is repeated until all the good items are finished. After this, the rest of the goods are sold in a process they call *kufagia* or sweeping (Kinyanjui, 2017).

Towards a Business Model

Conceptualising and constructing a business model is not an easy task. It requires understanding the context and the processes as well as the logic of the individuals involved. A business model entails identifying a customer, identifying what the customer values and delivering that value at an appropriate cost. Other factors that come into play include ethics, viability and sustainability. Development scholars' perspectives on peasants, traders and artisans are sceptical that the latter have a business model. For example, Scott (1987) in his studies of peasants in South Asia argues that peasants are not risk takers. In addition, they spontaneously respond to the animal instinct of survival and would rather be doing something else. Their production and exchange falls into the realm of moral economies.

Arguably, Wanjiku acknowledges that life is not a rehearsal (Kinyanjui 2014). She tries to make sense of and work with the conditions in which she finds herself. She creates communities, connects with others or taps into her networks. She does hard work and performs many activities, some of them precarious. She organises and sets rules and learns from the natural, socio-cultural and political environment. She learns from the past to predict the future. She uses principles of negotiation, collaboration and competition judiciously to arrive at a consensus. Punishment ranging from shame, isolation, and mob justice is applied to create a livable environment. Silence, secrecy or calculated revealing of information is used to safeguard individual or group interests. Verbal and non-verbal communication is also used. Through coded signs, she alerts her fellow workers of impending danger such as arrests. Ethics and morality are largely determined by what is experienced, seen, heard or workable or expected. Time (abstract, relative and real time) is also of essence in determining the business model. Prices may vary depending on the time of day or characteristics of the customers.

Wanjiku's model is an antidote to greed, cut-throat competition, inequality and survival for the fittest worldview that breeds conflict. Her model offers practical lessons on how self-regulating autonomous communities can work fairly and in harmony. Her model is the missing link that the modern economy needs to inextricably connect people to each other. It offers the new economy the tenet of inclusivity, self-reliance, solidarity, continuous learning, democratic governance, reciprocity, pooling of resources, redistribution of resources, gifting, role of the divine, social protection, individual and communal wellbeing.

Competition and Collaboration

Neoliberal economies observe that competition is good for business since it leads to innovation. Why is there not much change among traders, artisans and peasants? Why don't some businesses die due to competition? In Wanjiku's business environment, competition and collaboration take place at the same time. Achieng observes that sometimes, one will see women running to be the first when a boat arrives at the lake shore. This may be an indicator that they are competing but once they get to the boat and start haggling for prices, they speak one voice. Women in most cases have come together and acted for a common cause when a misfortune befalls one of their own. Competition on the other hand is evident because women compete against each other on the same platform.

Collaboration in business transactions is evident among women sorghum traders in Kakamega. They collaborate to face the local authority officials but compete when attracting customers. They unite in determining prices, quantities and measurements. The uniformity in pricing creates consensus in the transaction. Individual traders abide because of fear of being ostracised if they are framed as a spoilers of the market. In Gikuyu, a trader who goes against the rest *nī ahandagwo nīa rīangī* (the rest stand up against her).

Eunice Atieno observes that collaboration and competition exists among the women trading in fish at Usare beach. Women harmonise efforts and save resources and compete against each other on an equal platform. Lilian Anyango notes that there is justice and fairness. Once a fisherman comes with a boat, it is specified who the consignment in the boat belongs to. The rest can agree with the owner to share the fish. Rebecca Oyugi notes that the there is no favouritism or corruption in the Beach Management Office.

When women artisans are juxtaposed against the male gender and the county authority, the balance of fairness and power dynamic changes. Anne Wanjiku Kiunga observes that there is no justice and fairness because women are not recognised. It is a male dominated world (men are more than the women), in the cluster and women don't have a voice. In terms of elected seats, men get most seats hence denying women representation that can champion their interests. Kamukunji Jua Kali cluster for example, receives a lot of funds or assistance. Unfortunately, it is the men who benefit. In the absence of rules and regulations governing pricing for example, among the Tabaka soapstone dealers, some women felt that there was no justice and fairness. According to Jane Obita, some people fight for themselves and are not transparent. Jemimah Williams castigates dealers who set their own prices for the different products. As a result of this, Margaret Obadiah observes, competition is uneven and prices keep on fluctuating. The prices in the shop are the same as prices those carvers sell to wholesalers. It is important to note however that although these women are observing the lack of justice and fairness in pricing, they are still staying put in the business. Understanding fairness and justice among peasants, artisans and traders is not easy. It is complicated by many factors of state control and extortion by brokers. Equality is vital among the women dealing with sorghum farming. This can be witnessed when all the traders are given equal opportunity to trade, equal space, nobody is favoured more than the other. On the other hand, inequality arises when one is more favoured than the rest, i.e. well connected to the highest authority who accord them benefits or when traders use supernatural powers and witchcraft to do business. Traders who employ witchcraft to do business are usually castigated.

Redistribution

Redistribution of income and wealth is viewed as a strategy for overcoming inequalities and assisting vulnerable individuals. States initiate welfare programmes to support the vulnerable in society. Others provide pension schemes and unemployment benefits. Mkandawire (2006) argues that social policy is necessary for sustaining economic growth. In this light, some analysts argue that inequality and poverty can be arrested through redistribution policies. Ferguson (2015) in his book *Give Man a Fish* urges development practitioners and financiers to give financial aid to disadvantaged groups as a way of getting them out of poverty. He cites cases where financial aid has had positive outcomes to vulnerable groups. Some states distribute wealth through cash transfers, unemployment benefits, old age pensions, child support, disability allowance or basic income to vulnerable groups. Unfortunately, this form of redistribution of wealth is limited and far between in Kenya and most African countries. It is only recently that the Kenya government introduced cash transfer programmes as part of its social protection schemes to the elderly.

Peasant communities have a form of wealth redistribution that is not given the attention it deserves. Wanjiku redistributes wealth through gifting and reciprocity. This usually happens through support groups or households. Susan from Tabaka group says that transfer of money takes place within a household level when a parent grants his/her wealth or income to the children. Redistribution also takes place through the process of nurturing when women train their children about their business so that they can take after them in future.

Redistribution among women fish traders takes place within welfare groups where women contribute money on a daily basis to help them during the rainy seasons. Sorghum traders redistribute wealth through gifting and reciprocity. The women peasants, traders and artisans, take care of their parents, their children and themselves. They assist each other unconditionally until the other person starts engaging in productive endeavours and exchange.

Redistribution at the community level is also done through the *chama* and associations where one borrows money and repays it. It also happens through trainings. For instance, extension workers can be employed to take sorghum farmers through the sorghum farming cues for high and quality yields.

At the national level, redistribution is maintained through subsidies. Farmers are given subsidies and fertilisers (and even seeds) to encourage them to plant. In a humanist economy, where self-reliance and solidarity prevail, it is difficult to imagine a situation where one has no work, is unemployed or has to be dependent on others for survival. It is only in situations where some groups of people acquire property rights over the others that some are denied, and have no place to work to earn a livelihood in kind or in form of tangible goods.

Equality and Inequality

The configuration of state and local authority bylaws may collide with Wanjiku's perspectives of understanding inclusion and exclusion. This requires a delicate balance. For example, while there are set standards for the age when one should enter the world or work, in peasant, trader and artisan setting, children are part of production and exchange. Wanjiku's children accompany her to the farm or perform chores that support her business. A child may help the mother carry water for washing the cow's udders prior to milking, or the stool she is going to sit on while milking. Some artisan sites have age limits for entry. This varies from one market to the other. In the Tabaka group, children aged 18 years and below are not allowed to transact in soapstone production. In Kisumu, age limit is not a problem because of the level of poverty in the community. The majority of women who participate in fish trading are young ladies mostly in their early 20's. In Kakamega, business women allow children to participate in business. In general, it appears that women peasants, artisans and traders allow for Participation of everyone.

Most communities have gradually accepted women participation in monetised production and exchange. The society demands that women go out and work like men and provide for their families. Equality is paramount among the women dealing with soapstone in Tabaka. Everyone is given an equal opportunity to participate in the production process. The only difference is that some are more aggressive than others in conductng their business. Inequality may arise through favouritism, non-uniform pricing, or when one tries to use witchcraft to keep balance in social systems. Among the women fish traders, equality is maintained as long as one meets the requirements set by the Beach Management Office (BMO). Among the Kakamega sorghum traders, all the traders have an equal opportunity to trade and procure space. When the state usurps the responsibility of allocating resources or property, it may give to individuals who support it or those who bribe their way.

Reciprocity

Reciprocity is a social norm of responding to a positive action with another positive action. It relies on the expectation that people will return benefits for benefits and respond with either indifference or hostility to harm. When a customer is in need of a product that one does not have enough of, the trader or artisan directs them to another trader or artisan who has that product. One who has been given a customer also reciprocates when an opportunity arises. In a way, both parties benefit.

Among the Kisii Soap stone production artisans, it is not uncommon for them one to do something similar for each other in turns. Reciprocity is deeply rooted in everyday practices of women peasants, artisans and traders. It is part of their connectedness and interdependence. Among fish traders, when one is not feeling well, she asks a colleague to go to the beach and purchase fish and sell on her behalf. The latter is compensated. The one who does this is also accorded the same treatment when she is engaged. Among sorghum traders, people respond favourably to each other by returning benefits for benefits.

Solidarity Consciousness

Awareness of belonging to a group or community is a driving force for social, economic and political action. The evolution of peasants, traders and artisans' consciousness is somewhat taken for granted. Consciousness is built when people feel that they share a common experience, goals and destiny and are ready to collaborate to achieve their (collective and singular) aspirations. The following cases point to the existence of solidarity consciousness among women peasants, artisans and traders.

Among Tabaka soapstone artisans, there is unity, individualism and collective identity within the market. While people do their work, they share ideas on how to progress in the business. Sorghum traders come together and help their colleagues who are sick. Women team up to help themselves through welfares groups. They support each other during graduations, weddings and funerals. Solidarity consciousness is also enhanced by a battery of rules. These rules and regulations are created to facilitate smooth operations and harness individual agency. Eunice Atieno observes that the rules and regulations that regulate all the activities of the beach are formulated by the Beach Management Office (BMO) with the consensus of all the stakeholders. Grace Achieng notes that rules and regulations control crime, guide entry into trade as well as manage welfare activities. According to Lilian Anyango, it is a crime to fight. Newcomers must first visit the Beach Management Office for registration before being allowed to trade. All the stakeholders must contribute to the group welfare scheme. Drunkenness and disorderliness is not allowed. Cleanliness is mandatory. Fishermen must be in a company of two to three people in a boat to be allowed to fish on the lake.

Anne Wanjiku Kionga of Kamukunji Jua Kali cluster observes that rules govern individual behaviour and deal with interpersonal relationships. Members are not allowed to fight or make any unnecessary noise. According to Jacinta Wanjiru, one is not allowed to sell alcohol or be drunk on duty. One must fulfil her part of the bargain with the customer. No broking is allowed in Kamukunji Jua Kali.

Jane Obita observes that most of rules and regulations among Tabaka soapstone dealers are unwritten. No school going children are allowed to transact or be involved in soapstone in whatever level of production. Stealing is prohibited. Margaret Obadiah observes that no foreigner is allowed to buy the soapstone directly from the quarry or establish a company that will buy the soapstone directly from the carvers. There are no fixed prices for the products. According to Rebecca Samuel, when a customer visits a shop, the other shop owner should not interfere. Agnes Matitsa observes that the one is not allowed to light a fire inside the closed market using a *jiko* (charcoal burner). Every businessman is supposed to pay a ticket (Kshs 1,500). Stealing is not allowed. If one is caught stealing, he is arrested and handed over to county authorities.

Sorghum traders in Kakamega also have rules and regulations that govern them. According to Beatrice Achieng, one is not allowed to sell outside the restricted place. Abusive language is prohibited. Everyone must contribute to welfare. Susan Nekesa Wanjala observes that there is a committee that is mandated to come up with rules and regulations that govern the businessmen in Kakamega market. Rules represent all the views of the stakeholders in the market. Nancy Juma notes that payment for the stall (Kshs 2,500) should be done per month. One has to pay Kshs 10 to use the toilet and Kshs 30 to use the bathroom.

Among the Dagoretti plot owners, Rose notes that most of the rules define the relationship between the landlady and tenant. All rent payments must be made before the 10th day of each month. All payments are in form of cash. Cooking should not be done using electricity. Heavy alcohol drinkers are not allocated houses.

Women have attempted to come up with a business model that will help them articulate to global development. The model attempts to make Wanjiku's activities ethical and harmonious. Wanjiku's survival activities are not spontaneous. Her business model applies the principles of human economy such as sharing, reciprocity, learning by doing, redistribution, competition and setting of rules that govern the self and the group. Her economic model resonates with her orature, ideologies, norms and logic. The model helps her to perform her production, reproduction and consumption roles in an integrated manner.

Figure 2 is a diagrammatic presentation of women economic model. The women operate in a turbulent economic environment full of crises. They are at the mercy of stifling effects of government policy and competition from privileged formal businesses. The diagram shows the business embeddedness to Divine and physical forces. The belief that divine forces are in control provides the traders and artisans with the confidence to engage in business as well as accept outcomes.

The physical factors affecting women economic behaviour include the family and community. The family provides the traders and artisans with moral and monetary support for the business. The family launches one into business. The community also supports traders and artisans by providing ideas, finances, skill training or serving as customers. The family and community also serve as the yardstick for judging the success of individual traders and artisans using social economic indicators such as sharing and generosity.

The Women's business outcomes are not only measured by monetary value. They are judged by the way they are human. That is the way they carry themselves in society or how they take care of their children's education, parents' welfare, type of housing, contributions to church and community groups. Traders and artisans wellbeing is also judged by investment in real estates, plots, transport and animals in both urban and rural areas.

The business model is characterized by the embeddedness of business to personal, community and Divine domains. It is driven by the human spirit of self reliance, courage, endurance, resilience and hard work as well as by solidarity.

A PERSON AND THE ECONOMY

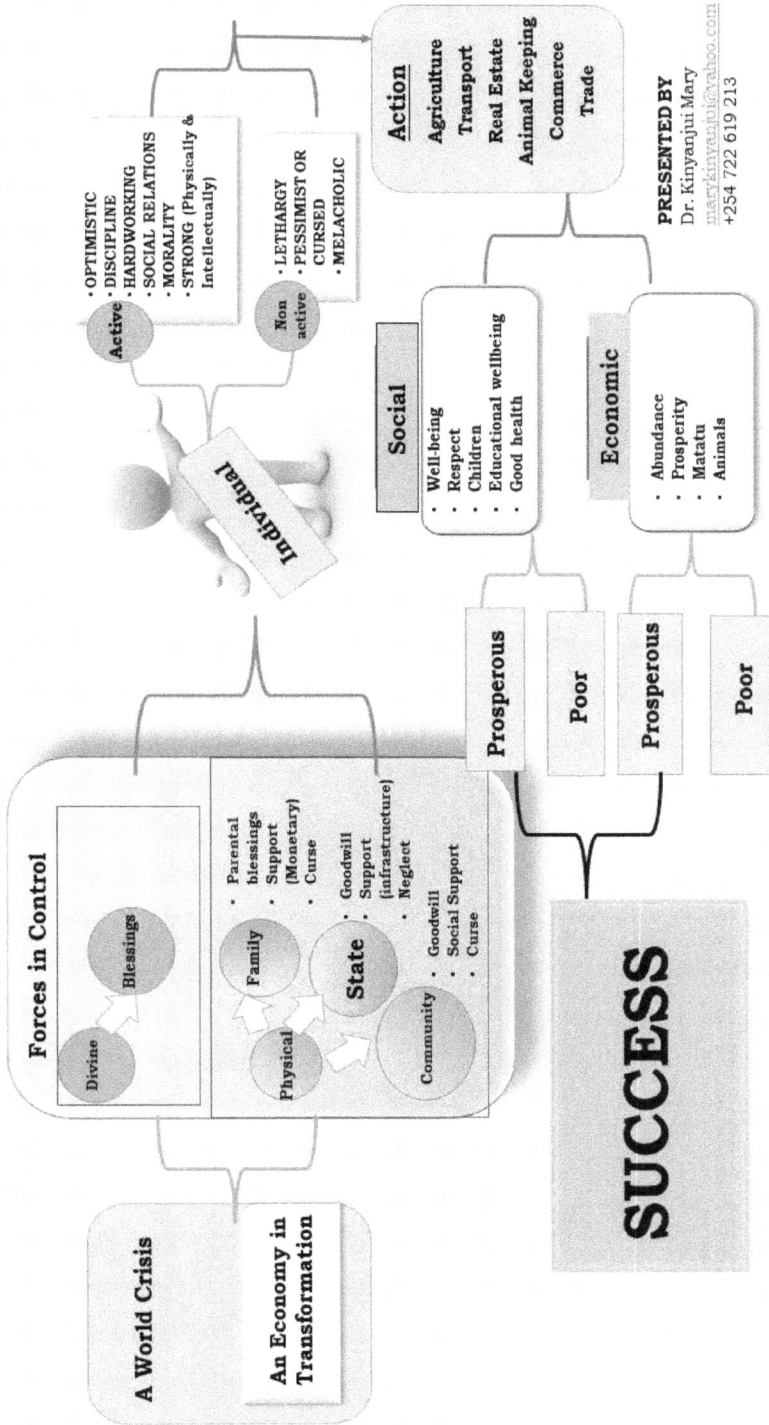

Individual

Active
- OPTIMISTIC
- DISCIPLINE
- HARDWORKING
- SOCIAL RELATIONS
- MORALITY
- STRONG (Physically & Intellectually)

Non active
- LETHARGY
- PESSIMIST OR CURSED
- MELACHOLIC

Action
- Agriculture
- Transport
- Real Estate
- Animal Keeping
- Commerce
- Trade

PRESENTED BY
Dr. Kinyanjui Mary
marykinyanjui@yahoo.com
+254 722 619 213

Social
- Well-being
- Respect
- Children
- Educational wellbeing
- Good health

Economic
- Abundance
- Prosperity
- Matatu
- Animals

Prosperous

Poor

Prosperous

Poor

Forces in Control

Divine → **Blessings**

Family
- Parental blessings
- Support (Monetary)
- Curse

State
- Goodwill Support (infrastructure)
- Neglect

Physical

Community
- Goodwill
- Social Support
- Curse

A World Crisis

An Economy in Transformation

SUCCESS

CHAPTER EIGHT

WANJIKU'S ATTEMPT TO CREATE PLACE IN HOUSEHOLD AND COMMUNITY

This chapter documents Wanjiku's attempt to create a place in her household and community. A flourishing family, self-reliance, and independence are important in Wanjiku's attempt to make her household and community. Wanjiku brings this to fruition from the money she earns from her undertakings that include the peasant trade and artisan activities. Her use of money is guided by the logic and norms of nurturing and connecting communities. Wanjiku views wellbeing in multiple dimensions. The dimensions include good health, good personal and family reputation, spiritual orientation, emotional consciousness, strong social relationships, meaningful and rewarding work and a thriving household and community.

Wanjiku also values catching up with peers' social and economic infrastructure and technology. Money is not valued for its own sake. It is first used to meet nurturing basic needs such as purchase of food, acquisition of medicine, buying of clothes, supporting parents, supporting siblings or meeting her children needs, including those for schooling. Money is also used in functions to connect community in form of church contributions, gifting in wedding ceremonies, gifting in graduations, payment of dowry, and meeting funeral expenses. Wealth is a sum total of the combination of these indicators of wellbeing. One is wealthy if she is a 'people person'. She has agency to meet personal and social and economic responsibilities in the household and in the community. Wealth is not about hierarchies in Wanjiku's perspective. It is about her ability to balance mutual interests in production, generosity and reciprocity in her place of encounter in the household and community.

Champions of women economic empowerment decipher the rationale for women economic empowerment and gender equity. Are we maintaining stereotypes of women as care givers and nurturers or liberating them from these stereotypes? After gender equity is realised, what is the ultimate goal of women empowerment and gender equity? What is the purpose of development? Feminists like Chimamanda (2015) argue that marriage upon which households, family and community are constructed is faulty because girls are socialised to marry and nurture while male children are not. This book does not intend to split hairs about feminism, or to determine what is good for women. It is out to document Wanjiku's view on monetisation and its impact on her wellbeing. What does Wanjiku do with her money? What does she advance? At what point should the state interfere with matters concerned in Wanjiku's place in the household and community? Some people argue that the state should intervene in social services such as schooling, health, and provision of jobs. Others argue that the state should not interfere with matters considered to be personal and domestic. In Africa, it is argued that individuals should cater for their health and education. Individuals inundated with the philosophy of self-reliance may or may not rely on the state for such goods. This spirit is best captured in the character Efuru in Flora Napwa's (1966) novel *Efuru* and the Protestant Church of East Africa's philosophy of *Jitegemee*. Gatu (2017) coined the term to free the church from dependence on financial support from England. Hart (1973) calls for an economy that provides for reproduction of human beings and sustains life in general. He argues that putting the wellbeing of people and communities at the centre, rather than the profits of banks and corporations, is the way to go. Wanjiku values a mode of economy that allows her to propagate and sustain her offspring. She puts the interests of her children at the forefront. She makes the household and community habitable and rich in human and interpersonal relationships. She invests in moral institutions such as the church that serves her spiritual needs. She is more likely to participate in building the church rather than a school. She believes that the local priest and the church maintain some degree of moral values that schools do not. Most schools do not adapt to local rules and regulations.

Personal, Household, Family and Community Wellbeing

Images of gloomy, tired and emaciated women dot development photographs, literature, films and documentaries to urge the world to rescue African women in general and peasants in particular. Such images have contributed to massive inflows of capital to developing countries, sometimes with little or nothing to show in development. This is well captured by Hancock (1989) who explains how global aid has become an industry that seeks to sustain itself instead of solving the problems it pupports to solve. The neoliberal world has made us believe that money and power define wellbeing. This ignores the fact that other indicators of wellbeing exist such as being rich at heart, being a people-person and contentment.

Wanjiku's personal and community wellbeing is reflected in her imaginary of human, social and physical infrastructure. Personal wellbeing is reflected in human development as well as the type of household infrastructure. It is also reflected in nurturing and connecting human beings. This is done through sharing, gifting and purchases that meet personal, household, family and community needs. To Wanjiku, money is useful if it is used to nurture and connect communities. Community wellbeing is reflected in the type of churches and schools available in the community A people's social imaginary is determined by their physical, human and divine experiences, as well as their norms and values. This in turn governs how money is used and circulated in meeting the social imaginary.

Grace Achieng's perspective of wellbeing is the ability to be sober, successful in business, and contented. Lilian Anyango, Rebecca Oyugi and Rehema Ongwen attribute wellbeing to good health and being at peace with oneself.

Wellbeing is also indicated by one's ability to perform functions such as nurturing or taking care of parents. Agnes Masitsa, Fransisca Atsango, and Beatrice Achieng find fulfillment in taking care of their children and parents. This brings about joy, less stress, and satisfaction that one has brightened the life of another.

Wellbeing is also viewed in terms of fairness and justice in the household and family. Ruth Aketch and Eunice Atieno observe that when everyone is given equal opportunity, this justice and fairness breeds fulfillment.

It is also viewed in terms of harmony. Lilian Anyango's entry into the culture of money has created a base for household and community harmony. If her husband is not able to meet family obligations for one reason or another, she is able to step in and fill the gap. If she doesn't have, he provides. This ability to pull together elicits harmony in the family and community. Rebecca Oyugi observes the same among the women fish traders in the community. Anne Wanjiku Kionga, Jacinta Wanjiku, Rhoda, Jemimah Williams, Mary Ombui, Rebecca Samuel and Rose also observe that harmony is a mark of wellbeing.

Women peasants, traders and artisans attempt to create a community that can enable them to harness human agency, transact, learn from each other and make rules that govern individuals and groups. The communities form a social relationship which serves as a basis for solidarity and social consciousness of belonging and sharing things and ideas in common. The consciousness is a basis for agency, solidarity, identity and resilience.

Jane Obita notes that solidarity has improved how she connects with other women. For instance, they share business ideas and travel experiences to enable them read from the same page. Solidarity creates a certain level of independence and confidence. Jemimah Williams notes that solidarity has strengthened her group bond.

Family, Household and Community

Through monetisation, Rhoda's position in the household, family and community has improved. She is able to meet personal and family needs. Fransisca Atsango is able to meet her daily personal and family needs. She can also donate to the church. She has also been assigned a role of counselling the youth in her church since she is a role model. Her profit has also been used to diversify into other areas such as animal husbandry. It is from Sorghum farming that Nancy Juma is educating her children, paying rental fees, supporting her parents, and contributing towards church. It is from sorghum farming that Agnes Masitsa has bought a piece of land and become a business mentor. Catherine from Dagoretti notes that her community participation has increased. She is active in church activities, participates in community fundraising, and has become an opinion leader in the community. Rose from Dagoretti observes that in spite of her status as a single parent, being a landlady has improved her social standing and given her confidence to participate in community welfare activities. From monetisation, Jane from Dagoretti has been granted leadership positions in the community. Mama Jua Kali of Kamukunji acknowledges that monetisation has made her purchase land, build several houses for herself. She chairs various women welfare groups and plays an activist's role which involves fighting for the preservation of Kamukunji. She was once elected Chairlady of Kamukunji Jua Kali Association in 2013. She uses her negotiating skills and experience to address constraints and regulations that affect artisans. She has defended fellow colleagues from law enforcement authorities.

Margret Obadiah observes that monetisation has enabled her meet her family's basic needs with ease, improved her status among fellow women and granted her the ability to invest. Monetisation has improved Mary Ombui's relationship with other women and increased her mobility and exposure. She has travelled to Kampala, Rwanda, Mombasa and Nairobi. Agnes Masitsa says that monetisation has improved her connection with other women, enabled her to meet family interests. Beatrice Achieng, Rebecca Achieng, Rebecca Samuel, Fransisca Atsango, and Susan Moraa all observe that monetisation has strengthened their bonds with fellow women, improved their social status, increased their proactivity, enabled them to own assets, and given them the ability to participate in household decision making.

Wanjiku's benefits of participation in peasant, artisan and trader activities are geared towards meeting goals related to the construction of her place in the household, family and community. This reinforces the fact that women's participation in global development is closely intertwined with their socially constructed roles of nurturing and connecting communities. Women's participation in global development enhances their self-determination and self-reliance in providing for the offspring in the household. It also enhances their connection with siblings and parents in the extended family through sharing with siblings or reciprocity in the case of taking care of parents. Monetisation also influences their positioning in the community such as being leaders of the local *chama* or church group. Their influence in community may be insidious but may include such activities as serving as reference points or mentors for younger entrants into the market. It may also extend to influencing political behaviour of peasants and artisans. They celebrate when they are able to take their children to school and when they are able to provide for the family. Monetisation is also a platform for single mothers to negotiate their position in the household or in the community. Single mothers are able to finance their everyday transaction and live independently. Women are also able to achieve harmony by supplementing the effort of their spouses to meet family needs.

The monetisation struggle is not just a matter of gender equity *per se;* it is also hinged on the fact that Wanjiku is able to provide and negotiate from a point of strength in the political economy of the household. This is a position that many women lost when men became the first to be monetised while their products were excluded from the circuits of monetisation through cash crops, education, indentured labour, or employment in government services and corporations. This implies that the gains from the work of peasants, artisans and traders cannot be just vanquished. Their logic, philosophy and ways of deploying surplus needs to be enfranchised. They contribute to personal liberty, access to basic goods, health and education which are integral for thriving households and communities. The investment in intergeneration transfer of knowledge is particularly important because it contributes to a thriving humanity as envisioned by Hart (1973) in his proposal of human economy. It is also bears testimony to the Bandung development vision of self-reliance, interdependence in fair and equal communities where everyone was given a chance to participate in human survival and enhance human dignity. Most of the women acknowledged that they had gained some respect in society because they were doing something for themselves, working in solidarity with others as well as sharing and giving in reciprocal relationships. The next chapter presents information on the way women monetise production and exchange in the household, build business, save and invest.

CHAPTER NINE

WANJIKU AND ACCUMULATION

This chapter provides information on how Wanjiku engages in self-reproduction in her production and exchange. It also demonstrates the efforts she makes to structure her business for continuity. Wanjiku endeavours to construct an economic system where families and communities thrive and flourish so that humanity can move to the next generation.

There is no agreement among scholars about which institutions, norms, values and logic should be used to position women in the economy. The majority of these scholars feel that taking women out of the household is the direct passport to economic empowerment and gender equity (UN Women, 1995). Some feminist movements argue that moving women from the household to the public domain would empower them economically and elicit gender equity. Some hold that the household activities such as nurturing and consumption do not lend themselves to women empowerment and gender equity. This is because nurturing activities are not paid for while consumption goods are brought into the household from outside from shops and supermarkets. More often than not, they are paid for by the male worker.

Women movements in Africa observe that poverty is feminised (McFerson, 2010; Kaka 2013; Ngunjiri, 2008). Women are said to be poorer than men for lack of land rights, cultural and patriarchal control of resources, corruption and lack of government policies to promote women economic empowerment and gender equity. Further, women are concentrated in low value economic sectors in the informal sector (Chen, 2001).

While the above observations make some sense, it should be noted that women are poor because of exploitation by global and local merchants. Global merchants have crafted economic models that dominate and control the production and exchange thatwomen engage in. For example, in grain and coffee production, their role in production and exchange is invisible in finished product labels manufactured by global and local merchants. The local and global merchants sell their technologies, seeds, pesticides and fertilisers at exorbitant prices. They regard their coffee beans as low value hence they add value and later on sell at exorbitant prices. The peasants seem not to get value for money as expressed by Dowden (2010) statement, 'our tip for the waiter for bringing us that coffee port will be more than a week's income for the family in Africa who grew coffee.' This statement clearly indicates the level of injustice in the global economy.

Women are however transforming the household and building wealth stocks. This is happening in female headed households (Chant, 2016). Women in female headed households engage in income generating activities that change their gender relations in the household. The ways women accumulate through household transactions, business, savings and investments raise the question on whether there is a feminist or womanist way of accumulation through production and exchange. Feminist geographers like Gibson-Graham *et al* (2013) argue that the end of capitalism will usher women into the political economy. They argue that women need to take back the economy from corporations. Community economies contribute to just, productive and sustainable global communities at the household, community and Nation. Gibson-Graham *et al* (2013) have developed models to create community economies based on feminist ideas. Kinyanjui (2012, 2014, 2019) has documented how ordinary people and more so women have used collective action to pool financial resources and use solidarity entrepreneurialism in an utu-ubuntu business model to move from the margins of production and exchange to the centre. Women have tapped (and continue to tap) from their feminine genius of solidarity to withstand oppressive urban and patriarchal rules and regulations in colonial and post-colonial Kenya Kinyanjui, (2013, 2014, 2019).

The next question that comes to mind is whether women have a universal feminist logic, norms and values of accumulation in household production and exchange transactions. Critiques of feminism especially those from non-Western European world have questioned whether women from different racial, ethnic, class, sexual orientation, religion, and cultural backgrounds can have universal values regarding socio-economic and political issues. Mohanty (2003) questions the universality of feminism since women from the non-Western cultures are viewed as victims, uneducated and tradition-bound. African American women like Alice Walker (1983), Hooks (2000) argue that White women have been oppressive to both African women and men.

Women, however, have more in common in matters of reproduction and production. They are all overwhelmed by patriarchy and the global capitalist mode of production. While much has been written about the brutality of white male in colonial Kenya, not much has been written about white women during colonial Kenya. For example, the Gikuyu term for white people *nyakeru* (white) or *muthungu* (one who shows outright abuse of privilege) are gender neutral. White women during the colonial and post-colonial eras represented a softer version of whiteness for example, Minnie Watson who founded a home to feed the Gikuyu in 1900 (Anderson, 1997). After the death of her husband, Minnie continued with her husband's mission work in Thogoto and founded a school for orphaned children during the day and an evening school for young adult males. Two white women, Karen Blixen (1937) and Mary Leaky present scenarios of white women in colonial Kenya. Karen Blixen (1937) in *Out of Africa* demonstrates her struggles and contradictions with dealing with white male patriarchy, fighting for Gikuyu land rights as well as the way to treat her male African workers. Mary Leakey worked alongside her husband discovering fossils in Northern Kenya. She also championed women education and a Girls' school is named after her. Joy Adamson in postcolonial Kenya worked in conservation works with her husband. She preserved and dried flowers from the African wild which are now displayed in the Kenya National Museum. Other women worked as nurses, teachers and assisted in their husbands' mission work in parishes. Catholic nuns started girls' schools and hospitals in different parts of the country. White and Asian women associations joined and worked together with African and Asian women under the association of East African Women League. Most educated Kenyan women who are fifty years and above were educated in girl missionary schools such as Alliance, Kahuhia, Tumutumu, Mary Leakey, St Francis, Loreto Limuru, Loreto Msongari, Kianda, St Mary's Igoji, St Mary's Bururu, Loreto Matunda, Ngandu, Mugoiri, Sacred Heart Kyeni, Precious Blood Kilungu, Kerugoya, Mlango, and Star of the Sea, where they had encounters with white female teachers or nuns. It is difficult to associate white women with the brutality attributed to white male colonialists. It is equally difficult to divorce it from them.

The first generation of African women writers, such as Ama ata Aidoo (1965), Grace Ogot (1966), Flora Napwa (1966) resisted the Western brand of feminism. They advocated for the recognition of family and motherhood as integral to femininity but not weakness. Other women writers like Margaret Ogola (1994, 2000) in *The River and the Source* and *I Swear by Apollo* have articulated the strong nature of women in character, work and education as well as the role they play in connecting humanity across generations and communities. Other African women writers like Wangari Maathai (2007) and Muthoni Likimani (2005) in their biographies observe that male structures in Africa are oppressive to women just as those espoused in Western feminism. Muthoni Likimani in her book *Fighting Without Ceasing* documents the effects of sexism in her home and work. In her endeavour to create a career and business, she encountered both oppressive African and white male discrimination.

In the light of the current global economic and socio-cultural transformations, Mohanty (2003) argues that indeed, what oppresses women is the global capitalist structures. She calls upon women to rise against capitalist structures. Most neoliberals, however, believe that there is no alternative to capitalism. This was confirmed after the demise of Soviet Union in the 1990s, they argue.

Wanjiku has, however, maintained an anti-colonial and anti-capitalist mode of production which embraces the family, community and the divine in transactions. She challenges the masculine frame of doing business which is unsupportive to women. This thuggish or male oriented approach has hindered most women to break the proverbial glass ceiling. They have to put in many hours in the workplace to the detriment of their home and family lives. This certainly calls for the search of women's economic model.

A society that encourages flourishing children and creation of human relationships is better than one determined by violent conflict and preoccupied by exploitative economic gain. There is a need for an alternative ethical code that is not necessarily determined by male ideologies and structures. Women start small business using a feminist production and exchange ethics informed by the feminine *utu*. The women peasants, artisans and traders construct their businesses in the household and market place using logic, norms and values of caring and connecting to community. They juggle with money in the contexts of gifting, sharing and reciprocity.

In the light of the above discussion, it appears it might be plausible to argue for a universal feminist or women model of monetising production and exchange. Regardless of colour, religion, race, and class, most women are engaged in reproduction and production in the household and community. The model could add to the already existing ones such as the ones documented by Hall and Soskice (2001) in their book *Varieties of Capitalism.* The duo demonstrate how different capitalist countries shape their type of capitalism by adopting different social and welfare policies. Japan's form of capitalism is different from the one in Germany, France, Great Britain or the United States. The capitalism in Latin American countries is arguably different from that of African countries.

Elumelu (2014) argues for a brand of capitalism called Africapitalism. This brand allows the private sector to play a critical role in the evolution of Africa's infrastructure. From Nigeria to South Africa, there is a new activism calling for the interrogation of African cultural practises that reinforce business management and practise. Such activities are going on at Wits Business School (the Graduate School of Business Administration at the University of the Witwatersrand, Johannesburg) or in the International Business Association conferences. Kinyanjui (2019) proposes solidarity entrepreneurialism or the *Utu-Ubuntu* business model that consists of individual and group agency, self and group regulation, and creation of communities for harnessing agency, interpersonal learning and socialisation into business ideas and deployment of surplus according to humanistic values.

Most of the current economic thinking points to the fact that the current global economy is not sustainable. It has contributed to high levels of inequality, poverty, unemployment, financial crisis, and collapse of housing and financial markets in most parts of the world. Some economies like Greece are on their knees riddled with heavy debts. There are also environmental problems such as global warming, deforestation and wanton mining that are threatening human life. In the context of these global economic uncertainties, women peasants, artisans and traders have stuck to their mode of production into the 21st Century. This model is working for them.

The dilemma in the management of the unsustainable global economy is reflected in the United Nations' 17 Sustainable Development Goals (SDGs). The goals are a reflection of the contradictions between sustaining the culture of money and self-regulating markets in the creation of a more equal society and the need for a just and fair society without compromising economic growth, the wealth of local and global corporations as well as their hegemonic power relations in the world. How can the conditions of gender, class, indigenous and subaltern conflicts as well as the natural environmental crisis occasioned by climate change be bettered when the economic ethic of individual self-interest and economic gain rules?

Human beings are in one life struggle that involves passing on the baton of all that is beautiful to the next generation with grace. One must live, work, and pass on the baton. This means having an economic ethic that is based on the need to create thriving and flourishing families, communities and nations with the sole aim of sustaining humanity. This calls for solidarity and collaboration with other human beings as opposed to cut-throat competition. Human beings are 'inextricably connected and interdependent on each other' (Tutu 1999). This relationship is expressed as 'I am because you are and because you are therefore I am.' In Zulu, this spirit is referred to as *ubuntu*. It is *utu* (humaneness) in Swahili (humanness) and *umundu* in Gikuyu. Human interconnectedness and interdependence are relevant and useful today in addressing the current global political economy architecture and infrastructure.

Women peasants, artisans and traders have handed over to the 21st Century global economy the tenets of the household as unit of production and exchange and the African marketplace. In the household and the African marketplace, the women use an economic model that allows the interplay between humanness, solidarity and economic wellbeing. Labelling this as failed development (ILO, 1972; Hart, 1973; Hyden, 1983; Chen 2001; Page 2012) would be to deny them their place and role as subjects of human and economic development in the global economy.

Women together with men have contributed to monetisation of transactions in the household, family and community within the logic of nurturing, sharing, gifting and reciprocity. Their understanding of wellbeing and wealth influences their daily transactions. They have sustained the principles of self-reliance, working for oneself and resilience. Peasant activities are not spontaneous or primitive. They are driven by a conscious mentality, values, ideas and structure.

The resistance by peasants, artisans and traders to pay levies has forced governors to change their stance on fundraising for their counties. Their resolute persistence and demand for space and opportunity has rendered many urban and regional planners of African cities helpless. Experts who teach individuals about the rules of good business start-ups, management and resilience have been left wondering as they see the sprawl and multiplication of peasants, artisans and traders in cities and rural areas in Africa. Wanjiku marches on without business plans, assembling factors of production, doing market research, investing in technology, advertising, selecting location wisely, enlarging the capital base through borrowing, registering a company, keeping records, and studying competitors among other elitist business demands. Wanjiku marches on without self-help books such as 'How to Become a Millionaire'; 'How to Get Rich'; 'How to Persuade Customers'; and 'How to Invest in the Stock Exchange.' Wanjiku marches on without being affected by the fact that most business start-ups do not live to see their fifth birthday in spite of tutorage from incubation and innovation centres. The latter die out like the fordist mode of production vanquished in Europe and North America.

Making of Households a Site of Monetised Production, Exchange and Investments

The following case studies illustrate the logic, norms and values behind women peasant, artisans and traders accumulation in the household and community. The cases also demonstrate how monetisation impacts on women's everyday life.

Peris Kibet, a trader in the Kimalel Goat Auction began selling honey in 2005 because at that time, goat business was down. Using money she got from her honey business, she was able to pay goat fees for the Kimalel goat auction, provide food, support her dependants and make church contributions which at the time were set at Kshs 3,000 or $30 dollar per woman. She was also able to pay the monthly contribution of Kshs 400 or $4 dollar required by her social group. She joined other women to form a *chama* that raised more money which they loaned to each other. In the cooperative, the women established friendships and supported each other in managing individual businesses. As the businesses grew, other responsibilities followed in the community. She became a church treasurer at St. Francis Catholic church. This responsibility was bestowed on her because she was now considered financially and socially stable. She started buying bulls which she would later sell at the auction when mature. She has diversified to tomato farming under the Molok and Eldume irrigation schemes. She continues selling honey and rearing livestock. She would rather keep animals than put money in a bank. Her money is balanced between buying honey, buying goats and meeting the needs of her children, especially education. "When I receive money, I prioritise school fees for children, buying honey to cater for off seasons and for farming. Personal, family and community flourishing is a continuous struggle and cannot rely on the goat auction alone because it is not always stable in returns," she says.

Jane from Dagoretti was given some rooms for renting by her father. She has been able to build two more on her own. She reported that her income was just enough for her and her children's use and therefore she had no surplus for investment. With improved resources and savings, she hopes to one day invest in the real estate, especially because the demand for houses is on the rise. Her strength lies in the frugal management of available resources and discipline towards investments as a sure recipe for her financial stability. She is proud of the fact that she is not dependant on anyone and that she does not borrow for her family upkeep. Besides the fact that she always has cash in her pulse, she also saves in the bank and via M-Pesa (mobile money facility). She also invests in welfare groups. She lives within her means and is grateful to God for enabling her to provide for her children well.

Catherine inherited her rental rooms from her mother. She spends the rental money on her household needs, maintenance of the rental houses and saves the rest of it. She hopes to purchase a plot from the savings. She hates being in debt and does not borrow from family or bank. She saves money in her church *chama* which is supposed to help single mothers to raise money and capital to invest in small business. She also operates an eatery. She feels she is financially secure because of her tangible assets. "Currently I have no fears about money as my plot and house are fixed assets and even if my eatery collapses, I will comfortably continue living," she says.

Rose raises income from her rental houses. She has some savings and is able to maintain her family. She hopes to raise enough money to purchase more parcels of land and build more houses. She is hopeful that her sons and daughters will assist in the investment and later become inheritors. Having money has enabled her to have control over her household affairs.Mama Jua Kali was able to enter into monetised production and exchange because her husband catered for household needs.

"Since my husband would cater for household needs from his salary, I diverted the money I had to business. From the profit generated from my business, we were in a position to buy parcels of land and build commercial rental quarters," she says.

She does not prefer to save money in the bank but prefers tangible assets. "I do save in a bank. The money that we save in a bank is for emergency. The rest of the money is used in the business or to buy assets. I would rather have more metallic goods to sell than to keep money in a bank."

Agnes Masitsa's ability to accumulate through household production and exchange transaction has made her financially independent and helped her to have command over her household.

"I don't depend on anyone. I have bought land from this and have other businesses running parallel to this one. I don't save money in a bank. Money saved in a bank doesn't have any benefit. I only save Kshs 20,000 to 30,000 or $200 to $300 dollar in a bank for emergency cases. I would rather re-invest back to my business," she observes.

Beatrice Achieng evolved from a sorghum retailer to wholesaler. She achieved this by reinvesting money back into business.

"I re-invested back to the business. That is how I grew fast to becoming a wholesaler," she says. She prefers to invest in in tangible commodities rather than have money in the bank. She has bought land and owns two motorcycles. She also saves money in a merry-go-round and *chama*. That is, she saves in solidarity with people she knows or are related to her.

Fransisca Atsango has been able to accumulate and diversify her household production and exchange transactions from her sorghum business. She ventured into poultry farming where she rears chicken. She is able to move money between the household and business in a manner that she meets her production, reproduction and nurturing roles.

"From the profit, I first make a budget in order of priority. Family needs, that is, foodstuff, clothes, shopping and school fees top the list. I plough back the remaining money to the business." She acknowledges that she will train her children on how to run the business. This will ensure continuity. She has accumulated assets through her production and exchange transactions in the household. Her purpose has been to meet family needs, re-investing into the business and pay back the loans which she borrowed from her social welfare group. She is elated to be facilitating the learning of her children.

Alice Akoth's accumulation is geared towards production and reproduction. "Apart from using the money I generate in investment, most of my money is used to meet my family's basic needs and medication," she says. She circulates her money between reinvesting in business and meeting family needs.

Grace Achieng's entry into accumulation is to meet her reproduction and nurturing roles. She meets her household needs such as paying of school fees and reinvests in the business. Jane Obita started with moderate investments in soapstone carving. Her investments have been growing steadily.

"From the soapstone production, I was able to purchase parcels of land and invest in the education of my children," she says. Like most of the other women, she prefers to stockpile soapstone rather than save money in a bank. She circulates her money between meeting household needs and reinvestment in business. She is independent and has control and command in her household. She has also developed self-confidence.

Jemimah celebrates her gains of her accumulation in production and exchange transaction by saying that her wealth lies in the success of her children. She has also invested in tangible commodities like buying pieces of land and building rental houses. Like most of the women she stockpiles her commodities rather saving money in the bank. "I value having more soapstone than investing in a bank," she says.

Like the rest of the women, she circulates her money between household reproduction and nurturing and reinvesting in business.

Margret Obadiah has benefited from accumulation through production and exchange in soapstone carving. What began as modest transaction has grown such that she has purchased parcels of land, she is able to pay school fees for her children; she has bought a public transport vehicle, she has a motorcycle and reinvests in business. She prefers to circulate money in different household and business transactions as opposed to saving in a bank.

"I don't believe in saving the money in a bank. I would rather purchase more soapstone and see them. Selling them would generate more money than having the money idle in a bank," she says. Susan Moraa accumulates to meet future reproduction financial transactions. "I have sold some of the parcels of land I had bought to service family needs. My family is big," she says. She would rather not save in the bank because, "banks have stringent conditions for borrowing a loan and they charge high interest." She circulates money between household transactions and those of the business. But most often, reproduction and nurturing roles override those of business.

"When I get money, I invest back to my business by going to the market to purchase more materials. The remaining money is channelled back to service household needs," she says. The above narratives illustrate that women accumulate in the household for purposes of reproduction, production and nurturing. They start with what is available or given to them by parents or inheritance. The women either accumulate through transactions within their household or at the marketplace. They can start out by renting rooms that are part of the family housing, selling honey which is harvested in the family beehive or sorghum grown on the farm. Some of their activities involve going against patriarchy. For example, Peris buys goats and bulls for sale in the goat and cow auctions. It can also involve building houses or engagement in carving which is a male responsibility. Some parents go against the cultural norms and allocate their daughters production and transaction activities or projects that will help them become monetised while others are socialised to take up responsibilities once they start reproduction by their mothers. The need to meet caring and nurturing responsibilities is an important logic for monetising household production and exchange. This means after giving birth and having children to take care of, women then think of how to meet the everyday needs of food, health and schooling. It appears that money is also directed to meeting basic needs for sustaining life and maintaining thriving household and communities. These needs include health, education, shelter, food and monetary security.

There is a close connection between spiritual affairs and the business and accumulation. They attribute success to in business to divine intervention while having more money allows them to participate in church activities. Some women take up greater responsibilities in church because they have more money. The business, the household, the community and the divine are closely connected. Money is circulated between the household, the business and community. In most instances women start with frugal resources. They juggle with the earnings to meet their reproductive and nurturing roles and at the same time plough back some money into production and exchange.

There is great resistance to capitalist money infrastructure and architecture such as banks. They prefer not to save money in the bank. They prefer to accumulate by purchasing tangible assets such as parcels of land, vehicles, motorbikes and houses. These tangible assets appreciate more in value than money in the bank. Money saved in the bank is for emergencies. The tangible assets can be easily be disposed-of when money is needed. In most instances, reproduction roles are given priority when allocating resources in the household. Care is also taken to ensure that money is ploughed back into business.

Saving money is also complex issue. It appears that the women prefer to stockpile goods rather than save money. This is partly due to the fact that saving interest rates are low. They also prefer to invest in the *chama*. Investment in the *chama* is solidarity based and is a form of sharing and collective action. The *chama* enhances their agency to participate in socio-economic and cultural action. It also enhances their sense of belonging to a community of traders, artisans and peasants. This in turn builds their agency in amidst precarious conditions. It is also a form of redistribution of wealth among the members. They also support each other during celebrations and mourning ceremonies. The *chama* is a site for learning, exchange of ideas and socialisation (Kinyanjui 2012). It is a tool for money circulation in the community of women peasants, artisans and traders. They pool savings and lend to each other at favourable interest rates. Money is circulated between the household and business as well in the *chama* and community especially in church. This method of circulating money resonates with the women's logic of gifting, sharing and reciprocity that is hinged on the women's reproduction roles.

Women's monetisation of transactions also creates independence and self-confidence which resonates with Chants (2016) observation that gender relations in households are being transformed. It is also in line with Kinyanjui (2014) argument that the household is the nucleus of production in the city for a large majority of informal economy workers.

The narratives reveal the need to target the household as the site of monetisation and accumulation through production and exchange. It demonstrates that the first step towards women financial inclusion may begin by accumulating through commodities that are within their reach. The significance of this is echoed by Anne from Githunguri who observes that although dairy farming may be seen as dirty, heavy, manual, and that she is not 'modern' like other urban women, she is better off than majority of them. From the sale of one single calf, she can raise Kshs 80,000 or $800 dollars. She has food from the farm. Her monthly milk earnings are far much greater than some of the urban wages some women earn in Nairobi. Another woman artisan in Kamukunji also intimates that her earnings are higher than those of women who work as clerks, secretaries, security, waiters or domestic workers.

The women accumulate horizontally rather than vertically. They measure accumulation through the tangible assets they have been able to accomulate or the other transactions they have been able to meet. They also measure their success by their ability to diversify or longevity in business. Success in business is also measured by having an inheritance to leave behind for their children. Being able to educate children is a key measure of success. Other indicators are being able to feed the family or provide family with medicines. This accumulation goal-oriented measure of business success may be different from the pure capitalist method of investing money to fetch more money and where profits are the measure of success.

These narratives of accumulation through production and exchange in the household clearly demonstrate that women peasants, artisans and traders have logic, norms and values for their everyday livelihood negotiations practises. This explains that the survival of this mode of production into the 21st Century is not spontaneous. It is maintained by logic, norms, values and structures based on solidarity or built into the household and community. Neoliberal elite development projects must address these elements (logic, norms and values as well as the way they are structured) in order to come up with measures to integrate them. These initiatives must incorporate the household and community and desire to continue life to the next generation. They must also address issues of solidarity transactions that involve gifting, sharing and reciprocity. This will involve coming up with a more humanistic model of development that is illuminated with logic and ethos of the feminine *utu* (humanness). Every child born must be nurtured and conditions created for them to thrive and flourish in the household and community. No child is lesser than the other. Women peasants, artisans and traders are not a failed development project. They engage in strategically crafted feminist models of production and exchange which are geared towards flourishing families and communities at the local level. They are not a *tabula la rasa* or spontaneous phenomena. It is because of the latter perspective that the development elite comprising governments, academics and development practitioners have failed to capture their mode of production.

CHAPTER TEN

CRAFTING A COMMUNITY ECONOMIC MODEL INCORPORATING WOMEN

A community can organically evolve or craft an economic model that facilitates its ability to thrive or flourish. The model can be insurgent (such as to counter conditions of domination and control); strategic (to achieve a desired end) or a human response for self-provisioning and advancing humanity to the next generation. Women peasants, artisans and traders use a mix of all the above. They sometimes rebel against the established order of things, rules and regulations. In this case, the community crafts economic models that are anti-patriarchy, anti-capitalist and anti-modernity in their transactions. Their household transactions and work are treated as cultural or social activities geared towards achieving humanistic goals rather than economic categories. The transactions and work are governed by rules of gifting, sharing and reciprocity. Investments and accumulations are geared towards the human response of self-provisioning and advancing humanity to the next generation.

This book has looked into the positioning of Wanjiku in the global economy by understanding her logic, methods, interpretation of wealth and wellbeing as she engages in neoliberal markets as a trader, artisan, and peasant. She transforms the household into a locus of monetised production and exchange transactions without compromising her non-commoditized reproduction roles and non-market social values of solidarity, gifting, sharing and reciprocity. The book has discussed her organic creation of self and group regulating markets.

The three methods of crafting community economic models that incorporate women logic, norms and values in transactions and organisation of labour are the Githunguri model, insurgency, control and domination.

Indigenous Models of Production and Exchange

Indigenous models of production and exchange take a variety of forms. They are mostly anti-patriarchy, anti-capitalist and anti-modernity. Communities persist in indigenous chicken breeding, sorghum trade and soapstone production. This preserves their identity and mode of production and exchange from modernity, the culture of money and self-regulating markets. Most of the production and exchange transactions are carried out through solidarity networks of family, friends and neighbourhood associations. They thus escape the government machinery of taxation and inclusion in the computation of GDP. It is the individual farmer who computes the value of her range chicken. The fisherfolk determine the value of the catch. Soapstone carvers also dictate the value of their craft.

Insurgency model

Women peasants, artisans and traders defy the household social order to participate in monetised transaction and create self and group regulated markets. This exercise is not easy. They have to break the ropes that bind at two levels: their household members and fellow colleagues at the work station. According to some women, their spouses never agreed on the kind of business the women were doing. The following are some of the reasons for the causes of conflict.

Incitement from the community: One respondent from Tabaka soapstone traders said that her husband was warned by his fellow males that if his wife became successful in business, she would desert him. He chased her away in advance but welcomed her back on realising that he had made a mistake.

Financial differences: Several women noted that most men were afraid that if their women became well-off, or financially independent, they would be disobedient. Some women reported that their husbands refrained from participating in meeting family needs such as provision of food and payment of school fees upon noticing that their wives were financially empowered. Some women thus decided to separate with and (in some cases)divorce their husbands. Other women observed that their husbands did not support their monetised production and exchange. Others complained that their husbands were over-protective and would spy on them.

One respondent from Kakamega, Nancy Juma, had to divorce her husband for being too suspicious whenever she would interact with male clients.

"I don't have a husband. I left my husband because of his behaviour. He knew very well that we did not have money and when I took the step to look for money through business, he would be paranoid whenever I transacted with men." According to another woman, "my delving into business generated a lot of conflict between my husband and I. I am not sure if he was incited by his fellow men. He took off with his belongings and married another wife."

Yet another woman observes that, "I think it is my soapstone money that caused my separation with my husband. He was a teacher by profession and was not interested with my soapstone business." According to another woman, "it is obvious that when a woman starts getting her own money, her family members and close relatives start giving her a lot of responsibilities in the house. When she asks why, conflicts arise."

The above cases demonstrate that sometimes it is not easy for women to enter into the sites of monetised production and exchange.

Extractive Models Crafted for Domination and Control of Peasants

Coffee production and exchange was one of the post-colonial strategies of monetising communities in central Kenya. The 1960s and 1970s were heydays of coffee production and exchange. In the colonial era, coffee farming was a preserve of the whites and the loyalists referred to as *ngati*. This was slowly liberalized and accessible to others. After the collapse of the international coffee agreement, coffee prices plummeted making most farmers to opt out of coffee farming in the 1970s. Some women peasant farmers who egged on continue to produce coffee in a volatile economic environment.

Prior to its downfall, Gatukuyu Coffee Farmers' Cooperative Society used to perform well and it received the admiration of many residents of these areas who planted coffee bushes as a major revenuegenerating activity of the household. The locals had learnt the ropes of coffee cultivation while working as labourers in European settler farmers' coffee plantations.

Coffee management was properly executed and the rewards were commensurate to the efforts that farmers put in. The leadership was based on the village quota system, ensuring proportionate representation of all the villages in the entire coffee cooperative society. Responsible leadership, transparency and accountability ensured that farmer revenues were remitted in a timely manner and in full. The first generation leaders of the society, although mostly illiterate, were honest, hardworking and safeguarded community interests.

The leaders that took over were literate but pursued individual interest. They were christened *njuhiga,* individuals who are knowledgeable but use their knowledge to serve their selfish interests. These disrupted the availability and timely deployment of farm inputs, disordered credit provision, rigged votes, were averse to periodical meetings, had poor public relations and politicised the cooperative. The cooperative management board was infested by politicians who had selfish interests and set up their own coffee marketing agencies that fleeced the cooperative members. The production went down. Women could not make ends meet from their coffee produce under these exploitative circumstances. This cooperative was different from Githunguri because of leadership, ethical conduct and commitment to community wellbeing

CHAPTER ELEVEN

CONCLUSIONS AND IMPLICATIONS

Of all of Africa's societal establishments, the least understood is probably the indigenous economic system. The "hunters and gatherers" tag has persisted, reinforcing the notion that either Africa had no economic institutions before contact with the Europeans and Arabs or the existing ones were inferior. Some quarters, arguing that subsistence farming was rife, erroneously hold that trade and exchange were unknown. While books on pre-colonial Africa have dwelt excessively on the modernist perspective which views Wanjiku's peasant and petty commodity production as primitive, backward and in need of transformation to fit in the modern global economy, some scholars amplify the Marxist perspective which claims that Wanjiku has been excluded from capitalist production.

Wanjiku's logic and motive

Wanjiku hails from mixed backgrounds in terms of ethnicity, age, education, marital status, location of business, and source of working capital. Economic informality for women is a socio-cultural logic of managing poverty and creating employment as well as a way of achieving inclusion in the urbanism project. Since economic informality is not counted in government statistics, the role of women and their contribution to the national economy remain invisible. There is a need to see the possibility of a city constructed on a platform of economic informality, stable households and human capital.

Wanjiku has not been idle, waiting to see things happen. She knows that life is not a dress rehearsal. It is a reality. She is not engaged in debates on life expectancy. This is because she is not expecting life. She is living the life. She knows that each day counts to improve her lot in life, as well as the lot of her family, relatives, community and ultimately the nation. She does not wait to be invited to a negotiating table to get employed. She scans her immediate environment, identifies the prevailing needs and seeks ways to offer goods and services. She is resilient, innovative and crafts strategies to circumnavigate adversarial policy and patriarchal hegemony. While she may start off disadvantaged, she strives to turn stumbling blocks into stepping stones to achieve fulfilment in life. Her provision of goods and services – hence her contribution to the national economy - may not be captured in government statistics, but this does not dampen her activities.

Wanjiku's solidarity and competition

Her entry into the monetised economy is largely enhanced by strong family, friendship and ethnic bonds. The act of skilling some and inviting others to join her mode of work is based on the African logic of mutual co-existence. Wanjiku invites neighbours, relatives or friends along, because they too have similar needs. These bonds explain why their businesses are situated in close proximity to each other, and often exhibit similar products. Wanjiku's marketplaces serve as nests of solidarity. Some individuals join the marketplaces as trainees and become skilled by learning on the job. Most become employers after they have accumulated enough skills and money to buy their materials. This explains the short employment durations. This dynamism generates a situation where the businesses do not grow vertically by increasing the number of employees but horizontally by increasing in numbers.

Wanjiku deploys what is akin to *ubuntu,* a philosophical concept from southern Africa that refers to the inextricable interconnections between all human beings. *Ubuntu* holds that all human beings occupy a single moral universe and share a moral sensibility that makes them recognise their duty to each other. *Ubuntu* espouses commerce with a human face to it. It is opposed to a system that rewards only a small elite. Cognisant of the fact that no one can live well in solitude and that one's actions impact on others, group agency that taps into each other's strength is embraced. Through the group agency, they pool their savings in a *chama* (cooperative), thereby enhancing their ability to afford certain kinds of transactions. Being part of supportive networks and engaging collaboratively in work is seen as a way to guarantee thriving.

It is not uncommon to find a husband and wife working together to grow in spite of their unequal power relations. The Githunguri SACCO, for example, encourages each of the spouses to have shares so that they can co-guarantee loans to each other. Husbands also allow their wives to own animals such as cows. This mutual agreement and trust is usually not based on signed certificates at the registrar of marriages. For some, it is based on the traditional rites of payment of bride wealth or the acknowledgement by both families that they have children and are husband and wife. Rights and trust are mediated in such a manner that when a husband dies, the clan meets and allocates resources to the widow. In Githunguri Dairy Cooperative and Gatukuyu Coffee Farmers' Cooperative, some of the women acquired shares after the death of their husbands. These women are now shareholders and can be paid dues.

Wanjiku, rather than commoditise her labour in wage labour markets such as in corporations and governments boardrooms, converts her household into a space for work, production, exchange and consumption. Her logic of participation in the household economy is to ensure survival and concomitant thriving families and communities. Most of the social and economic activities that ensure human survival and thriving communities are closely tied to the household. The household is not only a nurturing and caring space, it is also a space for work, production, exchange and consumption. Socio-economic activities are constructed around the household. Most often, she starts her businesses with small amounts of money. She would rather work for herself. Wanjiku is thus able to control her labour and monetisation of production and exchange.

Wanjiku's ethic and trust

Wanjiku's business ethic exists on the basis of the human logic of nurturing. The contrast between the spread of capitalist global production and exchange with the peasants, traders, and artisan production can be compared to two variant graphical presentations. The global capitalist economy has two mouths, one in front and the other at the back. The mouth in front devours everything that comes before it. The one at the back devours things that come behind it or those that might escape the front mouth. The global capitalist spread encounters Wanjiku whose mode of exchange and production is like that of brooding mother hen sitting on several eggs. Once hatched, she feeds and gathers the chicks under her wings to keep them warm until they reach maturity. Once the chicks mature, she disperses and scatters them to be on their own. It is this sense of nurturing that sees Wanjiku involved in paying school fees for children, helping her ailing parents, assisting the disadvantaged such as widows, and ensuring that basic household needs are catered for. Githunguri Dairy Cooperative has, in part, been built around Wanjiku's values and needs. It is in this respect that it has tried to address household dynamics by ensuring that women have grocery stores where they can pick food on credit. The cooperative also gives loans for school fees. The cost of these goods is charged to the monthly milk earnings. This ensures that household needs are met before male spouses get their pay. Production and exchange is thus integrated with the women's logic of nurturing and connecting communities.

Wanjiku also aspires for self-fulfilment and actualisation. Her entry into the money economy boosts her self-confidence, inspires her agency, and enables her to negotiate from a point of strength. She experiences fulfilment when she is able to supplement family income, invest in real estate, build a capital base, diversify and inspires her immediate community.

It should be noted that Wanjiku's idea of wealth and wellbeing is not in hoarding material wealth. Wellbeing is viewed as good health, good personal and family reputation in a household and in the community, spiritual stability, emotional consciousness, as well as having strong social relationships in the household or community. Catching up with peers' social and economic progress, technology, production and exchange as well as strengthening the human value of work contribute to one's wellbeing. In sum, well-being consists of whatever builds the human self, and dictated by one's standing in the household and community. Thus, money is basically used to meet nurturing needs such food, medicine, clothes, children's education; supporting parents or siblings, and supporting communal functions such as church contributions and gifting in ceremonies such as weddings, graduations, dowry negotiations, rites of passage and funerals. One is wealthy if she is a people person; and if she has agency to meet personal, social and economic responsibilities in the household and in the community. Wealth is not about sovereignty and hierarchies. It is about being able to balance mutual interests in production, generosity and reciprocity in their household and community spaces.

In terms of labour relations, Wanjiku works collaboratively with the rest to grow crops, raise livestock and market goods. At times, communities pool their labour in groups. They also pool their resources in social groups where they share seeds, cuttings and suckers and cushion each other against socio-political and economic shocks.

Wanjiku's business model has struggled to coexist with the capitalist ethos which reveres individualism and lauds survive for the fittest, smartest and the most intelligent. Wanjiku's model encourages the logic of interdependence, self-reliance and community mindedness. It is this aspect that enables entrepreneurs to share spaces and transaction costs, decide together on which risks to take and which to avoid, and invite others to join them in their businesses. Every action is illuminated by a sense of solidarity.

While competition in capitalist communities is cut throat, Wanjiku's form of competition is different. Wanjiku competes and at the same time collaborates with those she works with. As a result, Wanjiku's businesses do not die out as the case in capitalist businesses. Women fish traders may run to be the first when a boat arrives on the shore. This is an indicator of competition. However, once they get to the boat and start haggling for prices, they speak in one voice. Women sorghum traders in Kakamega collaborate to face the local authority officials but compete when attracting customers. They unite in determining prices, quantities and measurements. The uniformity in pricing creates consensus in transactions.

Redistribution of income and wealth is viewed as a strategy for overcoming inequalities and assisting vulnerable individuals. While states distribute wealth through cash transfer, unemployment benefits, old age pensions, children support, disability allowance or basic income to vulnerable groups, Wanjiku has a form of wealth redistribution that is not given the attention it deserves. Wanjiku redistributes wealth through gifting and reciprocity. This usually happens through support groups or households. It can be through a parent granting his/her wealth or income to the children, training children to take after family businesses, contributing money on a daily basis to help during the rainy seasons, gifting and reciprocity. Taking care of parents, children as well as other people to engage in productive production and exchange is also a form of redistribution. Redistribution at the community level is also done through the *chama* and associations where one borrows money and repays it.

Wanjiku upholds economic justice. Anyone is free to sell goods in a market space and those with artisanal skills can sell their wares at manufacturing sites. Relations between workers and employers are based on a reciprocal system of fairness. Importantly, all activities are carried out openly, which helps to minimise injustices such as hoarding, unfair trade terms, overpricing, undercutting and exploitation. When one is sick, the other can purchase goods and sell them on her behalf. One trader can be sent to purchase goods on behalf of the rest. Economic justice is also seen in redistribution. The configuration of state and local authority bylaws may collide with Wanjiku's perspectives of understanding inclusion and exclusion. For example, while there are set standards for the age when one should enter the world or work, in Wanjiku's setting, children are part of production and exchange. Wanjiku's children accompany her to the farm or perform chores that support her business. A child may help the mother carry water for washing the cow's udders, or the stool she is going to sit on while milking. Some artisan sites have age limits for entry. In the Tabaka group, children aged 18 years and below are not allowed to transact in soapstone production. In Kisumu, age limit is not a problem because of the level of poverty in the community. A majority of the women who participate in fish trading are young ladies mostly in their early 20's. In Kakamega, business women allow children to participate in business. Equality is paramount among the women dealing with soapstone in Tabaka. Everyone is given an equal opportunity to participate in the production process. Among the women fish traders, equality is maintained as long as one meets the requirements set by the Beach Management Office (BMO). Among the Kakamega sorghum traders, all the traders have an equal opportunity to trade and procure space. When the state usurps the responsibility of allocating resources or property, it may give to individuals who support it or those who bribe their way.

When a customer is in need of a product that one does not have enough, the trader or artisan directs them to another trader or artisan who has that product. One who has been given a customer also reciprocates. In a way, both parties benefit. Among the Kisii soapstone artisans, it is not uncommon for them to do something similar for each other in turns. Reciprocity is deeply rooted in Wanjiku's operations. It is part of her gesture of connectedness and interdependence. Among fish traders, when one is not feeling well, she asks a colleague to go to the beach and purchase fish and sell on her behalf. The latter is compensated. The one who does this is also accorded the same treatment when she is engaged. Among sorghum traders, people respond favourably to each other by returning benefits for benefits.

Tabaka soapstone artisans share ideas on how to progress in the business. Sorghum traders come together and help their colleagues who are sick. Women team up to help themselves through welfares groups. They support each other during graduations, weddings and funerals. Solidarity consciousness is also enhanced by a battery of rules.

Wanjiku also creates rules and regulations to facilitate smooth operations and harness individual agency. In the fish trade, there are rules and regulations that regulate all the activities of the beach. They are formulated by the Beach Management Office (BMO) with the consensus of all the stakeholders. The rules control crime, guide entry into trade as well as manage welfare activities. In Kamukunji Jua Kali cluster, the rules govern individual behaviour and deal with interpersonal relationships. In Tabaka soapstone trade, they regulate who to participate in trade and how to carry out transactions. They also regulate payments towards the group, hygienic standards to observe, and environmental consciousness.

Johnson (2012) argues that Africans do not save, but rather store money in large sums and use it bit by bit. She describes villagers she got to know who did not consume their entire harvest in one year. They preserved goods and produce for the longer term and in case of emergencies. This is Wanjiku's mode of saving. They save in granaries. Traditionally, goats owned by one household were periodically sent to a neighbour's homestead for safe keeping. After some time, the goats are returned with new offspring. In this way, communities preserve and share their best breeding stock. Johnson argues that this kind of preserving and conserving is different from stockpiling goods for disposal via a stock exchange when prices are good. To a large extent, similar norms, values and logic about sharing and conserving can be observed in Wanjiku. Wanjiku often pools her resources to insure one another in a kind of crowd-funded group insurance.

Wanjiku acknowledges divine intervention. In the marketplaces, the interplay between the social, economic and spiritual domains is always evident. No individual is separable from the business or the business from the household. Both exist within the grace of a higher power. Wanjiku thus engages in prayer before embarking on business and resigns to God's will in her ups and downs. Her belief that divine forces are in overall control provides her with the confidence to engage in business and to accept business outcomes rather than resort to despondency, despair and blame games.

While engaging in the economy, Wanjiku resists practices she considers to be detrimental to her culture. The resistance is propagated through orature, the unwritten word that is passed on through families in chats, narratives or songs. Wanjiku attempts to transform by adopting principles and tenets of capitalist production and modernity that are in harmony with her cultural practices. This move towards cultural preservation has a bearing on the preservation of cultural commodity production activities. In the Luo cultural ceremony, it gave peasants, artisans and traders an opportunity to display their artefacts, regalia, pottery, traditional foods and brews. The increased sources of finance such as venture capital, microfinance, internet investments and credit schemes are vehemently resisted through various anecdotes and narratives. that instil fear and encourage individuals to accumulate their own funds and fund their transactions rather than become indebted. Wanjiku greatly resists capitalist money infrastructure and architecture such as banks. Rather than save money in the bank, she accumulates by purchasing tangible assets such as parcels of land, vehicles, motorbikes and houses. These tangible assets appreciate more in value than money in the bank. Money saved in the bank is for emergencies. The tangible assets can be easily be disposed-of when money is needed. In most instances, reproduction roles are given priority when allocating resources in the household. Care is also taken to ensure that money is ploughed back into business.

Wanjiku has been trying to assert her ethical business model in postcolonial Kenya. This model is based on solidarity in production and exchange, as well as in humane nurturing, connecting the logic and norms of well-being and wealth in the household and the community. Wanjiku can contribute to the global economy this mode of production that is human being centred, based on solidarity and that attempts to achieve balance between fetching money and creating families and communities where humanity can thrive and flourish. We need to learn from her economic model if we are to realise a sustainable, resilient, and inclusive global economy.

Wanjiku's exchange and production transactions is embedded in the person, community and the divine. The person and household become centres of production and exchange while the surplus is reinvested into the household and community pool. Educating children, buying land and acquisition of food and medicine are part of the household and community flourishing. Community affairs are also important. Through *vyama*, Wanjiku caters for community needs such as funerals, weddings, graduation and health concerns. In the divine realm, she prays for blessings and links success and failure to the divine. She invests in churches as part of her civic engagement. She has resisted mass consumption and rise of corporations as envisioned in global capitalism. She has upheld the right to work and do something for herself rather than work as servile labour in global corporations or civil service.

Solidarity prevailing over individuality in entrepreneurial encounters is an inclusive form of development that is uniquely African inspired by *ubuntu* logic, norms and values. Thinking about sustainability of world economies requires a world view that embraces collective engagement and resilience, since ūta merithitie ndatigaga kūhanda (One whose seeds have not germinated should not stop planting). Other tenets in the ubuntu world view include justice, self-reliance, human dignity and self-determination through the principle of 'I am because you are and because you are, therefore I am.' It means embracing every one and working together since we are inextricably connected to each other or 'we are family like a giant tree' as expressed in the American film Dream Girls.

Who is going to lead the *utu-ubuntu* movement of solidarity and collective action for a sustainable global economy? Wanjiku will lead this move since she has incorporated its tenets in her postcolonial accumulation experience as in the organisation of Kamukunji metalworkers, Dagoretti Plot Owners, Githunguri Dairy Farmers' cooperative, Saccos and *vyama* of fish, sorghum, soapstone and free-range chicken traders and peasants. They harness human agency and configure production and exchange in the context of socio-economic justice. Their logic and norms influence use and value of money, understanding of humanity and community, personal and communal well-being, wealth and civic engagement in the household and community.

Wanjiku's economy, also known as the informal or indigenous economy, has existed for generations. Despite the fact that it is frowned upon by many local and international economic experts, this unregulated self-reliant economy that has survived many formalisation attempts, portends tremendous hope if it can be tweaked to participate in local and global development. It is worth noting that formal businesses have attempted to borrow from it. For example, New Deep West Resort, a resort situated in Nairobi West area in Kenya adopted an African-Italian architectural design. Kikwetu Restaurant in Kisauni, Mombasa pioneered a cultural revival by selling traditional food predominantly. Most clubs in the country have embraced theme nights where guests are treated to Wanjiku's cultural activities. Safaricom, arguably Kenya's most successful company with both local and foreign ownership has given all its products and advertisements a Kenyan image utilising the beauty of the Kenyan landscape and used local terms and concepts in naming its products such as Mpesa, Sambaza and Bonga Points to mention a few. Learning from the traditional economy, the Safaricom company sells airtime in small denominations, enables monetary transactions in small quantities and colocates retail outlets. East African Industry or Unilever also adapted to Wanjiku's consumption habits through the Kadogo (small economy) by packaging cooking oil, soap, salt and margarine in affordable small quantities. Equity and Cooperative banks have also designed products tailored for actors in the informal economy. The banks have left high-end streets and gone to where Wanjiku works from. It is imperative that efforts be made to preserve the useful and enduring elements used by Wanjiku just like other aspects of the African cultural heritage. Equity Bank has developed products to suit Wanjiku such as lending to her using tea and coffee receipts which she was anticipating. Safaricom in its mobile banking platform embraced how Wanjiku shares in reciprocal relationships and introduced products like Fuliza a microloan programme that operates like the credit card in the West. Other products include Mshwari that have embraced Wanjiku's ways of managing money.

REFERENCES

Adesina, J. O. (2008). 'Archie Mafeje and the Pursuit of Endogenity: Against Alterity and Extroversion.' Africa Development Vol XXXIII No 133-152.

Adichie, N. C. (2015). We Should All Be Feminists. New York: Harper Collins.

Aidoo, A. A. (1965). The Dilemma of a Ghost. Harlow: Longman.

Aidoo, A. A. (1977). Our Sister Killjoy. London: Longman.

Anderson, G. H (1997) Biographical Dictionary of Christian Missions. NewYork. McMillan Library

Andole, O. H., & Matsui, K. (2019). 'Social Attributes and Factors Influencing Entrepreneurial Behaviours Among Rural Women in Kakamega County, Kenya.' Journal of Global Entrepreneurship 9 2 1-10.

Baringo County (2013). Baringo County Report. Baringo: Baringo County

Blixen, K. (1937). Out of Africa. London: Putnam

Booth, D., & Cammack, D. (2013). Governance for Development in Africa: Collective Action Problems. London: Zed Books.

Boserup, E. (1970). Women's Role in Economic Development. London: Allen Unwin.

Bromley, R. (1978) 'Introduction – The Urban Informal Sector: Why is it Worth Discussing?; World Development 6 (9–10): 1033 – 9. http://dx.doi.org/10.1016/0305- 750X (78)90061-X.

Brycenson, D. (2000). Disappearing Peasantries? Rural Labour in Africa, Asia and Latin America. (ed.) 2000. London: Intermediate Technology Publications, 333 pp.

Bryceson, D. (1995). Women Wielding the Hoe: Lessons from Rural Africa for Feminist Theory and Development Practice. (ed.) 1995. Oxford: Berg Publishers, 282 pp.

Bryceson, D. (1997) Farewell to Farms: De-Agrarianization and Employment in Africa. (ed.) 1997. Aldershot: Ashgate, 265 pp. (with Vali Jamal).

Burbank, Ke. (1994) 'A Survey of NGOS as Small Business Agencies in Kenya'. Working Paper No. 493. Institute for Development Studies: University of Nairobi

Busia County (2013) Finance and Amendment Bill. Busia. Busia County

Caretta, M.A., & Cheptum F. J. (2019). 'Enacting Feminist Countertopographies: Border Crossing Through Participant-Led Results Dissemination.' ACME: International Journal for Critical Geographers 18 1 23-48.

Chant, S. (2016) 'Women, Girls' Poverty: Empowerment, Equality or Essentialism'. International Development Planning Review 38 (1) 1-24

Chant, S., & Pedwell, C. (2008) Women, Gender and the Informal Economy: An assessment of ILO research and suggested ways forward. Geneva: International Labour Organization (ILO).

Chen, M. (2001). 'Women in the Informal Sector: A Global Picture: the Global Movement.' SAIS Review. Vol. 21 Issue 1.

Chen, M. A. (2012). 'Informal Economy: Definitions, Theories and Policies.' WEIGO Working Papers. No. 1.

Collier, P. (2007). The bottom billion. London: Oxford University Press.

Dalton, G. (1972). 'Peasantries in Anthropology.' Current Anthropology 13 3-4 382-415.

Demirguc-Kunt, A., Klapper,L., & Singer, D. (2017). 'Financial Inclusion and Inclusive Growth: A Review of Recent Empirical Evidence.' Policy Research Working Paper Series 8040. Washington: The World Bank.

Dowden, R. (2010). Africa: Altered States, Ordinary Miracles. London: Public Affairs.

Elumelu, T. (2014). 'The Rise of Africapitalism.' The Economist, November, 13, 2014.

Fanon, F. (1961). Wretched of the Earth. New York: Groove Press

Federici, S. (2012). 'Feminism and the Politics of the Commons in the Era of Primitive Accumulation.' In Federici Silvia (ed) Revolution at Point Zero, House Work, Reproduction and Feminist Struggle. Michigan Thomson Shore 138-171.

Ferguson, J. (2015) Give Man a Fish: Reflections on the New Politics of Distribution. Durham: Duke University Press.

Ferrand, D. (1999). Discontinuity in Development: Kenya's Middle Scale Manufacturing Industry. Unpublished PhD Thesis. University of Durham: UK.

Ferrand, David (2013). 'Building Inclusive Financial Markets.' In Ledgerwood, J, Earn, J. Nelson Candace. The New Microfinance Handbook: A Financial Market Perspective. Washington: World Bank

Fibaek, M. and Green, E. (2019). 'Labour Control and the Establishement of Profitable Settler Agriculture in Colonial Kenya.' Economic History of Developing Regions. 34 1 72-100

Foucault, M. (2002).Archaelogy of Knowledge. London: Routledge

Gatu, J. (2016). Fanning the Flame: A Story About a Man's Long Life in Church. Nairobi: Moran Publishers.

Gibson-Graham, *et al.* (2013). Take Back the Economy: An Ethical Guide. Minneapolis: University of Minnesota Press.

Gibson-Graham, J.K. (2006). Postcapitalist Politics. Minneapolis: University of Minnesota Press.

Ginkel, R. and Henkes, B. (2003) 'On Peasant and Primitive People's Moments of Rapprochement and Distance Between Folkore and Anthropology in the Netherlands'. Ethnos 68 112-134

Ginkel, R. V., & Henkes, B. (2003). 'On Peasants and Primitive Peoples: Moments Rapproachment and Distance between Folkore and Studies in Anthropology in the Netherlands'. Ethnos. 68 1 112-134.

Giugale, M. (2014). Economic Development: What Every One Needs to Know. Oxford: Oxford University Press.

Government of Kenya (2007). Kenya Economic Survey 2007. Nairobi: Government Printer

Government of Kenya (2007). Kenya:Vision 2030. Nairobi: Government Printer.

Guha, R. (1983). Elementary Aspects of Peasants Insurgency in Colonial India. Durham: Duke University Press.

Gyimah, P. and Boachie, W.K. (2018). 'Effect of Microfinance Products on Small Business Growth: Emerging Economy Perspective.'Journal of Entrepreneurship and Business Innovation.Vol. 5, No. 1.

Hall, P.A. and Soskice D. (2001). Varieties of Capitalism: The Institutional Foundations of Comparative Advantage. Oxford University Press.

Hancock, G. (1989). Lords of Poverty: The Power, Prestige, and Corruption of the International Aid Business. New York: Atlantic Monthly Press.

Hart, K. (1973). 'Informal income opportunities and Urban Employment in Ghana.'. The Journal of Modern African Studies. Vol. 11 No. 1: 61-89.

Harvey, D. (2010). The Enigma of Capital: and Capitalism Crises. Oxford: Oxford University Press.

Hooks, B. (2000). Feministm is for Everybody: Passionate Politics. Boston: South End Press

https://www.unaids.org/en/regionscountries/countries/kenya

Hyden, G. (1980). Beyond Ujamaa in Tanzania: Underdevelopment and an Uncaptured Peasantry. London.

Hyden, G. (1983). No Shortcut to Progress: African Development in Perspective. Oakland: University of California Press.

ILO. (1972). Employment, Incomes and Equity: A Strategy for Increasing Productive Employment in Kenya. Geneva: ILO.

Johnson, S. (2004). 'Milking the Elephant: Financial Markets as Real Markets in Kenya'. Development and Change. 35: 247–274. doi:10.1111/j.1467-7660.2004.00351.x

Johnson, S. (2012). The Rift Revealed: The Search for Financial Inclusion in Kenya and the Missing Social Dimension. Paper presented at the Institute for Development Studies, University of Nairobi.

Kaka, J. E. (2013). 'Poverty is a Woman Issue in Africa'. IOSR Journal of Humanities and Social Issues. Vol 18 Issue 6 77-82.

Kakamega County (2018). Kakamega County Integrated Development Report 2018-2022. Kakamega: Kakamega County.

Kamau, J. (2015). 'How Ruthless Coffee Mafia Enslaves Kenya.' Daily Nation, Nov 16, 2015.

Kamau, P., Bateganya F., Ilembo B. (2012). Culture and Women in the Lake Victoria Fish Trade: A Value Chain Analysis. End of Year Two Report Submitted to VICRES Secretariat, Inter-University Council for East Africa.

Kenya Gazette Supplement (2013). Micro and Small Enterprises Act. Nairobi: Government Printer.

Khandker, S. Khalily, B., Khan, Z. (1994) Is Grameen Bank Sustainable. Human Resources Development Operations Policy. HRO Working Paper. No 23.

Kiambu County (2017). Kiambu County Annual Report. Kiambu: Kiambu County

Kinyanjui M. N. (2019). The Sweet Sobs of Women in Response to Anthropain. New Castle Upon Tyne: Cambridge Scholars Press.

Kinyanjui, M, N. (2016). 'Ubuntu Nests and the Emergence of an African Metropolis'. Singapore Journal of Tropical Geography. 37 418-431

Kinyanjui, M. N. (Forthcoming). 'Mama Jua Kali: Female Resistance and Resilience to Coloniality of Modernism and Neoliberalism in Nairobi.' Special Issue. Journal of Language, Entrepreneurship and Technology Urban Affairs.

Kinyanjui, M. N. (1992). 'Finance and Availability of Capital for Small and Medium Sized Enterprises in Central Kenya.' Journal of East African Development and Research. Vol. 23. Pp. 63-87.

Kinyanjui, M. N. (2002). 'Peasant Organisations in the Development Process: Opportunities and Constraints'., Iin Romdhame, Mahmoud Ben and Moyo, Sam. (eds) Peasant Organisations and the Democratisation Process in Africa, Dakar:CODESRIA. Pp 293-313.

Kinyanjui, M. N. (2010). 'Social Relations and Associations in the Informal Sector in Kenya'. UNRISD Social Policy and Development Paper No. 43. Geneva: United Nations Research Institute for Social Development (UNRISD).

Kinyanjui, M. N. (2012). 'Trade Justice: The Case of Bonded Small Scale Farmers in Eastern and Southern Africa.'. In Musyoki, A. and Khayesi, M. (eds) Environment, Society and Development in East and Southern Africa, Essays in Honour of Professor Michael Kwesi Darkoh. Bay Press.

Kinyanjui, M. N. (2012). Vyama Institutions of Hope: Ordinary People's Market Coordination and Society Organization Alternatives. Nairobi: Nsemia Publishers.

Kinyanjui, M. N. (2013). 'Women Informal Garment Traders in Taveta Road, Nairobi: From the Margins to the Centre.' African Studies Review. Vol. 56(03) 147-164.

Kinyanjui, M. N. (2014). Women and the Informal Economy in Urban Africa: From the Margins to the Centre. London: Zed Publishers.

Kinyanjui, M. N. (2015). Coffee Time. Cameroon: Laanga Press.

Kinyanjui, M.N. (2015), Coffee Time. Bermenda. Laanga Press

Kinyatti, M. (2019). History of Resistance in Kenya. South Carolina: CreateSpace Independent Publishing

Koech, F. and Kipsang W. (2017) 'County Sets 30 Million Target for Kimalel Goat Auction'. Daily Nation, December, 19, 2017

Lewis, A. (1954). Theory of Economic Growth. London Routledge

Likimani, M. (2005). Fighting Without Ceasing. Nairobi: Noni Publicity.

Lorenzetti, L. M.J. Leatherman, S., Flax, Valerie L. (2017). 'Evaluating the Effect of Integrated Micro Finance and the Health Intervention: An Updated Review Evidence'. Health Policy Planning 32 5 732-756.

Lugones, M. (2010). 'Toward a Decolonial Feminism'. Hypatia Vol. 25 No.4 742-759.

Maathai, W. (2007). Unbowed. New York: Anchor Books.

Mafeje, A. (1981). 'On the Articulation of Modes of Production'. Journal of Southern African Studies, 8(1): 123-138.

Mafeje, A. (1991). The Theory and Ethnography of African Social Formations: The Case of the Interlacustrine Kingdoms. Dakar: CODESRIA Books Series.

Mafeje, A. (2003). The Agrarian Question, Access to Land, Aand Peasant Responses in Sub Saharan Africa. Geneva: UNSRID Civil Society and Social Movements Programme Paper No 6.

Magothe, T.M., Okeno T.O, Muhuyi, W.B., KahiA.. K. (2012). 'Indigenous Chicken Production: Current Status'. World's Poutlry Science Journal 68 119-132

Mahajan, V. (2008). Africa Rising: How 900 Consumers Offer More than You Think. New Jersey: Pearson Prentice Hall.

Mazrui, A. (1986). 'On the Concept We are All Africans'. American Political Science Review. Vol 57 1 88-97.

Mbataru, P. (2016). 'Direct Coffee Trade for Kenya: Who is Fooling Who?;. The Standard Newspaper. January 4, 2016.

Mboya, T. (1970). The Challenge of Nationhood: A Collection of Speeches and Writings. New York: Praeger Publishers.

Mcferson, H.M. (2010). 'Poverty Among Women in Sub-Saharan Africa: A Review of Selected Issues'. Journal of International Women Studies, 11(4), 50-73.

Mcferson, H.M. (2010). Poverty Among Women in Sub Saharan Africa: A Review of Selected

Mensah, B.O., &Wangai, P.N. (2011). 'Factors that Influence the Demand for Credit Among Small Scale Investors: A Case Study of Meru Central'. Research Journal of Accounting [Online] Vol. 2 (2). www.iiste.org.

Messah, O.B and Wangai, P.N. (2011) 'Factors that Influence the Demand for Credit Among Small-Scale Investors: A Case Study of Meru Central District, Kenya'. Research Journal of Finance and Accounting. 2 74-101

Mitullah, W.V. (1999). 'Lake Victoria's Nile Perch Fish Cluster: Institutions, Politics and Joint Action'. IDS Working Paper 87, Brighton: IDS, 1999.

Mkandawire, T. (2010). 'Running While Others Walk: Knowledge and the Challenge of Africa's Development'. LSE Online.

Mkandawire, T. (2014). 'The Spread of Policy Making and Economic Doctrine in Post Colonial Africa'. African Studies Review. 57 01 171-198.

Mkandawire, T. (2015). 'Neopatrimonialism and the Political Economy of Economic Performance in Africa: Critical Reflections'. World Politics Vol. 67 3 563-612.

Mnyamwezi, R. 2017 ' Kenyan Traders on Taita Taveta Border Complain of Harrassment by Tannzanian Authorities'. The Standard Newspaper. November, 26th 2017

Mohanty, C. T. (2003). 'Under Western Eyes Revisited. Feminist Solidarity through Anticapitalist Struggles'. Sings Winter. 500-534.

Moser, C. (1978). 'Informal Sector or Petty Commodity Production: Dualism or Dependency in Urban Development'. World Development 6 9 1041-1064.

Mullei, A., &Bokea, C. (1999). Micro and Small Enterprises in Kenya: Agenda for Improving the Policy Environment. Nairobi: I.C.E.G.

Mwatha-Karega, (1997). Rural Women in Small Business: Entrepreneurial Group Activities in Kitui District, Kenya. Unpublished PhD Thesis, University of Reading.

Namusonge, J.S. (1999) 'Entrepreneurship Development'. In Andrew, M. and Bokea, C. (eds) Micro and Small Enterprises in Kenya: Agenda for Improving Policy Environment. Nairobi: International Centre for Economic Growth

Napwa, F. (1966). Efuru. London: Heinemann Educational Books.

NCCK. (1969). Who Controls Industry in Kenya: A Report of a Working Party. Nairobi: East African Publishing House.

Ndegwa, D. N. (1969). Report on the Commission of Inquiry Public Service Structure and Remuneration Commission. Nairobi: Government Printer.

Ndikumana, L., Boyce J.K. (2018). 'Capital Flight From Africa: Updated Methodology and New Estimates.' Political Economy Research Institute. Amherst: University of Massachusetts.

Ndungu, M. (2011)The Massacre: 58 Years Ago Today that Still Divides Lari. Daily Nation

Ngunjiri, F. (2008). 'Corruption and Feminization of Poverty in Sub Saharan Africa'. JENDA, Journal of Culture and African Women Studies No 12.

Ngwala, T.A. (2011). Planning Development Challenges of Micro Retail Shops in Luthuli Avenue of the Central Business District of Nairobi. Unpublished BA planning research project, University of Nairobi.

Njoroge, K. (2016). The Decline of Spiritual Authority in Gikuyu Traditional Authority. North Charlestone: Create Space Independent Publishing Platform.

Nyeko, M. (2014). 'The Banana Eater.' In Allfery Wakatama Ellah Africa 39: New Writing from Africa South of Sahara. Bloomsbury.

Ochunu, M. E. (2013). 'African Colonial Economies: State Control, Peasant Manoeuvres and Unintended Outcomes'. History Campus. Vol. 11 1 1-13.

Ogola, M. (2004). The River and the Source. Nairobi: Focus Books.

Ogot, G. (1966). The Promised Land. Nairobi: East African Educational Publishers.

Onyambu, M. and Akama, J. (2018) Gusii Soapstone Industry: Opportunities, Challenges and the Future. Nairobi: Nsemia Publishers

Opondo, M. (2005). Humanising the Cut Flower Industry: Controlling Reality of Flower Production for Workers. Nairobi.

Oyeronke, (1997). The Invention of Women: Making African Sense of Western Discourses. Minneapolis: University of Minnesota Press.

Page, J. (2012). 'Industrialization and Economic Transformation of Africa: Introduction and Overview'. Journal of Africa Economies.

Vol. 21 (2012) Issue 2 1 ii3-ii18   https://doi.org/10.1093/jae/ejr049 Oxford University Press.

Podlaschuc, L. (2009). 'Saving Women: Saving Commons'. In Ariel Salleh (ed) Eco-Sufficiency and Global Justice. Pluto Press.

Polanyi, K. (1994). The Great Transformation. New York: Farrar and Rinehart.

Ravazi, S. (2009). Gendered Impacts of Liberalization: Embedded Liberalism. London: Routledge.

Roberston, C. (1997). Trouble Showed the Way. Women and Men in Trade in Nairobi Area 1890-1990. Bloomington: Indiana Press.

Rodrick, D. 2011 Globalization Paradox: Democracy and the Future of the Economy. New York: W.W. Norton

Rono, J.K. (2002). 'The Impact of The Structural Adjustment'. The Journal of Social Development in Africa. Vol. 17 No. 1.

Roy, A. (2010). Poverty Capital: Microfinance and the Making of Development. London: Routledge.

Sachs, J. (2008). Common Wealth: Economy for a Crowded Planet. London: Penguin Press.

Santos, M. (1979). Shared Space: The Two Circuits of the Urban Economy in Underdeveloped Countries. London: Routledge.

Sen, S. (2000). 'Towards a Feminist Perspective: The Indian Women Movement in a Historical Perspective.' Policy Research Report. Gender and Development. Working Paper Series- No. 9.

Shabbir, M.S. et al (2016). 'Impact of Social Media Applications on Small Business Entrepreneurs'. Arabian Journal of Business and Management Review 6: 203. doi:10.4172/2223-5833.1000203.

Soto de Hernando (2003). The Mystery of Capital: Why Capitalism Triumphs in the West and Fails Everywhere Else. New York: Basic Books.

Stiglitz, J. (2010). Free Fall: America, Free Market and the Sinking of the World Economy. New York: W.W. Norton Company.

Stuart, E., Samman, E., and Hunt, A.(2018). 'Informal is The New Normal: Improving the Lives of Workers at Risk of Being Left Behind'. Working paper number 530. London: Overseas Development Institute.

Thiong'o, N. (1977). Petals of Blood. Heinemann, London.

Thiong'o, N. (1986) Decolonizing the Mind: The Politics of Knowledge. Sulfolk: James Currey.

Thiong'o, N. (2016). Secure the Base: Making Africa Visible in the Globe. Cambridge University Press.

Thurston, A. (1987) Small Holder Agriculture in Colonial Kenya: The Official Mind and the Swynnerton Plan. African Studies Centre. Cambridge Monograph.

Todaro, M. P. (1994). Economic Development (5th ed.). New York, London: Longman.

Tutu, D. (1999). No Future Without Forgiveness. New York: Image Books.

UNWomen 1995 Beijing Platform of Action Turns 20.New York: UN.

Vakkyil, J. (2017). Resistance and Integration: Working with Capitalism at its Fringes.IÉSEG School of Management, Lille and Paris.

Wairia, N. C. 2006 'Githunguri Cradle of Independent Schools'. Kenya Beyond 2005

Walker, A. (1983). In Search of Our Mother's Garden: Womanist Prose. Harcout Brace Jovanovich.

Wallerstein, I. (1974). The Modern World System: Capitalist Agriculture and the Origins of the European World-Economy in the Sixteenth Century. New York and London: Academic Press.

Wallerstein, I. (1980). The Modern World System II: Mercantilism and the Consolidation of the European World Economy. New York: Academic Press.

Wallerstein, I. (1989). The Modern World System III: The Second Era of Great Expansion of the Capitalist World-Economy, 1730s–1840s. San Diego: Academic Press.

White, L. (1980). The Comforts of My Home: Prostitution in Nairobi. Chicago: University of Chicago Press.

Wilson, C. (1952). Before Dawn in Kenya. Nairobi: English Press.

Yimga, J. (2018). Micro Finance and Its Effect on Cost Efficiency. The Quarterly Review of Economics and Finance. 69 2015-216.

www.ingramcontent.com/pod-product-compliance
Lightning Source LLC
Chambersburg PA
CBHW030850270326
41928CB00008B/1302